AMERICAN CHILDHOODS

A Series Edited by James Marten

Small Strangers

Small Strangers

*The Experiences of Immigrant Children
in America, 1880–1925*

MELISSA R. KLAPPER

Ivan R. Dee

CHICAGO 2007

www.ivanrdee.com

Library of Congress Cataloging-in-Publication Data:
Klapper, Melissa R.
    Small strangers : the experiences of immigrant children in America,
1880–1925 / Melissa R. Klapper.
        p. cm. — (American childhoods series)
    Includes bibliographical references and index.
    ISBN-13: 978-1-56663-733-6 (cloth : alk. paper)
    ISBN-10: 1-56663-733-3 (cloth : alk. paper)
1. Immigrant children—United States. 2. United States—Emigration and immigration—19th century. 3. United States—Emigration and immigration—20th century. I. Title.
    JV6453.K53 2007
    305.23086'9120973—dc22

                                                          2006036831

Lovingly dedicated to my nephew Dovie Fine,
whose great-grandparents and great-great-grandparents
were once immigrant children themselves

Contents

Preface

THIS BOOK is an account of the experiences of immigrant children during the mass immigration to the United States from approximately 1880 to 1925. Immigrant children are defined here as those whose childhood and adolescence were centrally shaped by immigration and adaptation to the United States, whether they were born abroad or in America. These children came from all over the world, from Mexico and Japan and Canada as well as the more commonly considered late-nineteenth- and early-twentieth-century embarkation points of southern and eastern Europe, before restrictive U.S. legislation closed the floodgates in 1924. They took part in one of the most significant transnational movements of people in history: the arrival of nearly 25 million immigrants in the United States. Although children never constituted anything approaching a majority of these millions, child immigrants and the American-born children of immigrants made up an important part of turn-of-the-century American society. They have been largely ignored by the historical literature, yet their varied experiences embody the ways in which the related processes of immigration, urbanization, and industrialization molded modern America.

Even more than adults, children lived in worlds shaped by expectations: social, cultural, and familial. They experienced the world through a set of limitations on their choices based on their age. Because much of the historical record of childhood was actually produced by adults—either to establish conventions or to recall things past—the available documentation must be viewed with a great deal of suspicion. But certain patterns of the way age worked in people's lives do emerge. It is possible to know what children's lives were like and even to understand how they experienced their youth and what they did to shape it.

Immigrant children and adolescents were acute observers of their parents, siblings, teachers, community leaders, and peers. Whether they grew up in crowded tenements, insular mill towns, rural ethnic enclaves, or middle-class homes, the children left valuable records of their lives, as did their parents, teachers, social workers, and religious leaders, and other adults they encountered. Because a more expansive immigration history includes Mexican, Asian, and Canadian children as well as their European counterparts, *Small Strangers* reflects the geographic diversity of immigrant children. An abundance of memoirs, diaries, oral histories, and periodical literature reveals diverse ethnic groups, nationalities, and places.

That so many of these sources are in English reflects the frustration of immigrant parents who were unable to sustain their native languages, a condition much remarked upon in the ethnic press at the turn of the century. In many cases, ethnic periodicals themselves began to publish in English within a single generation. Despite the nearly universal presence of language and cultural schools in ethnic communities, immigrant children learned quickly and thoroughly that their success in America would be linked to their command of English. Even those who spoke their native language at home usually presented themselves in personal narratives in English, as Americans.

Small Strangers makes no claim to provide a theoretical outlook on the historical experiences of immigrant children in turn-of-the-century America. Instead this book combines a synthesis of existing material on immigration with original research focused on children's own perspectives. Culling as vast a body of literature as that of immigration history is a daunting task. Few existing studies pay much attention to children except as symbols of the struggle to acclimate to a new life and of families' success or failure in their new land. But the importance attached to immigrant children as symbols is highly significant. Their status deeply influenced their actual lives. Social workers and educators, for instance, decided soon after mass migration began that most Americanization efforts beyond teaching English to foreigners should aim at children. This structural decision affected every facet of real immigrant children's lives, from their educational and work opportunities to their family relationships. They did not choose the structure, but they did shape their own reactions to it. As immigrant children came of age, they were increasingly caught between the "traditional" and the "modern"—that is, they were confronted within their families and ethnic environments by both Old World expectations and New World demands. Many children made their own choices as individuals rather than as members of family units, an indication of the impact of the American ethos of individualism on their lives. This book examines these lived experiences in order to recreate the world of immigrant children and the role they played in creating, sustaining, and altering that world.

To reflect the centrality of the children, *Small Strangers* is organized according to the phases of their lives. This life-cycle approach allows for a broad comparison of ethnic and immigrant groups of children who had common experiences and faced common challenges. Few of these children were so sheltered at home that they tried to replicate a traditional Old World life they were unlikely to remember well, if at all. Similarly, few children were completely cut off from any sense of ethnic tradition or customary practice. Arriving in the United States just as mass youth culture was emerging, they found it both easier and more difficult than their parents to adapt to life in a country so foreign. In obvious ways, such as generally learning English faster and better than adults, the process of adaptation was easier for them. In more subtle ways, such as reconciling the contrasting expectations of parents, teachers, and employers, they found the process of adaptation more difficult. Immigrant children carried the burden not only of their own hopes for life in a new country but also those of their families, who typically measured success in America by their children. Their age and stage of life affected their response to all these challenges. Virtually all the children, for example, resolved the conflict between work and education by heeding the demands of the family economy. Tracing an issue like this one through a life-cycle approach demonstrates that the balance between education and work generally shifted as immigrant children approached adolescence.

Among these children, adolescents make up a particularly interesting group of historical subjects, since the conflicts they experienced grew stronger as they neared autonomy. One way to approach them is to examine the parallels between adolescence and acculturation, both of which embody moving from one stage (of life and of social integration, respectively) into another. The moment of transition reveals all the pushes and pulls involved with the process, especially the ways in which moving forward always meant leaving something behind. Modernization is neither inevitable nor necessarily positive; there are gains and losses within all cultural exchanges. The parallel is not perfect. It was often harder and less positive to leave behind centuries of tradition and a supportive nexus of family, community, and religion than to say goodbye to childhood. Still, adolescence was when many of these decisions were made. It thus provides a standpoint from which to examine the changes and continuities of life in late-nineteenth and early-twentieth-century America. Most immigrant adolescents wanted to make decisions for themselves. That freedom to choose, though sometimes illusory, for most of them was the very definition of America.

Many of the most iconic images of immigration to the United States during the late nineteenth and early twentieth centuries are of children: industrious Greek boys wearing caps and selling newspapers, dutiful Jewish girls minding their baby brothers and sisters on the streets where they lived, adolescent Mexican migrants stooping over crop fields, and nervous Italian siblings feverishly cracking nuts in family workshops. All these historical figures and more participated in a population movement that strained, challenged, and transformed American society and culture at the turn of the century. Just as the children's experiences represented the fulfillment or failure of their parents' expectations for a new life in a new home, so too does their history embody the complicated processes of acculturation and Americanization. *Small Strangers* tells the stories of these children whose youthful encounters with ethnic heritage, American values, and mass culture contributed to the shape of the twentieth century in a United States still known symbolically around the world as a nation of immigrants.

Acknowledgments

I HAVE a confession to make: I still read children's books. I like to read them, and I like to discuss them with my friends' children whenever I have the chance. Perhaps I should say that I read them from the perspective of a scholar with academic interests in the history of childhood and youth, and to some extent that is true. But mostly I read them because I enjoy revisiting old favorites and finding new ones. I read them because the sense of wonder that pervades good (and even not-so-good) books for children is something I hope always to bring to my own work and life. Although I did not realize at first what a herculean task I was taking on in writing this book, I have been continually delighted and, yes, filled with wonder at the complexity, diversity, and sheer humanity of the history of immigrant children.

Long before I joined the roster of authors writing books for the *American Childhoods* series, I was fortunate to be influenced by two teachers with deep commitments to the history of childhood and youth: Peter W. Bardaglio at Goucher College and Philip Greven at Rutgers University. I am grateful to them both for encouraging my interest in the subject and demonstrating its importance to the understanding of the past. A number of other guides have offered their support as I have worked on *Small Strangers*, including Joyce Antler, Dianne Ashton, Riv-Ellen Prell, Jonathan D. Sarna, Jonathan Zimmerman, and, most especially, Alice Kessler-Harris, who remains a peerless mentor and font of wisdom.

I am delighted to thank publicly all those who offered specific help along the way. James Marten, the editor of the *American Childhoods* series, has been a model of patient and encouraging support throughout the writing, revision, and publication process. Ivan Dee responded promptly and helpfully to all my questions. Two of my Rowan University students, Krystle Gnatz and Jeneen Abed, provided invaluable aid with photographic and bibliographic research, respectively. Jay and Gail Chaskes kindly made available a treasured family photo. My Rowan colleague Emily Blanck read the entire manuscript at a critical juncture, offering judicious comments that greatly improved the book. The participants in the Rutgers Center for Historical Analysis 2004–2005 seminar on the history of childhood, led by Rudy Bell and Ginny Yans, pushed me to think with greater clarity about the issues involved with comparative and interdisciplinary work. My department's Works in Progress seminar also provided a venue for advancing some of my ideas. I am fortunate to work with such an enthusiastic, dedicated group of colleagues.

Librarians and archivists at Arizona State University, the Bancroft Library, Bryn Mawr College, the Free Library of Philadelphia, Haverford College, the Historical Society of Pennsylvania, the Jewish Theological Seminary of America, the Library of Congress, the New York Public Library, and the University of Washington offered their services with courtesy and smiles. The staff members of Rowan University's Campbell Library, particularly the Inter-Library Loan Department, were unfailingly helpful and speedily responded to even my most obscure requests for research materials. Extra financial support for this book came from the Historical Society of Pennsylvania's fellowship program and Rowan's College of Liberal Arts and Sciences, which provided both release time and supplementary funds.

Last, but certainly not least, I want to thank my friends and family. Rivkah Fischman and family, Devorah Taitlebaum, Sarah

Gersten and family, Janet and Danny Eisenberg and kids, Sara Esther and Yaakov Kader, Judith and Barry Levitt and kids, Malka Miriam Mandel, and Marsha and Mike Wasserman are constant sources of friendship and warmth. Even in the last stages of her final illness, Stephanie Sherman encouraged me to tell her stories from the book. She and Moshe, along with their children, are perpetual inspirations. Ashley Klapper, friend and cousin, has been listening to me talk about this book for a long time and has always responded with helpful interest. In the process of writing this book, I learned more about my own family history from Arnold and Edith Klapper, Marjorie Mitchell, and Beattie Broide. I am especially grateful for the love and support of my sister and brother-in-law, Jennie and Josh Fine, and my parents, Ferne and Mitchell Klapper, who graciously continue to provide a home for the books that were such an important part of my childhood.

M. R. K.

Merion Station, Pennsylvania
January 2007

Small Strangers

CHAPTER ONE

Childhood and Immigrants: Changing Ideas at the Turn of the Century

————

If mankind is to be reformed or improved, we must begin with the child. This Exhibit has been organized to show what has already been done for children, and to demonstrate the importance and necessity of doing much more along this line. . . . Those who enjoy the benefits and share the responsibilities of our cities must plan for the children, for, although they are our youngest citizens, they are potentially the most important.

—Cyrus H. McCormick, 1911[1]

❧ WITH THESE WORDS, the philanthropist Cyrus McCormick in May 1911 opened the Chicago Child Welfare Exhibit. Twenty thousand to 45,000 people attended the exhibit daily to visit the displays, model classrooms, and conference proceedings comprising one of the proudest moments of the Progressive Era. The three major sections of the Child Welfare Exhibit highlighted the home, private philanthropy, and public programs, reflecting reformers' beliefs in public/private interactions and the need for both individual and state reform efforts. All the popular programs related to children that progressive reformers had established, from juvenile courts to widows' pensions to housing reform, were on display at the exhibit. Images of bereft children with no parents, playgrounds, or future, captioned "In Need of Friends," encouraged visitors to become friends of children, first by reforming their own practices toward children and then by becoming involved in local, state, and national child-welfare activism. Theme days spotlighted specific groups of children, such as "The Foreign Child." Much of the rhetoric of the exhibit, including McCormick's opening address, assumed that urban children were nearly synonymous with foreign children.

By the time of the Chicago exhibit, a significant demographic shift resulting from the huge growth in immigration during the late nineteenth and early twentieth centuries was almost complete. In 1860 there were four million foreign-born persons in the United States, but by 1920 there were nearly fourteen million.[2] Neither of these figures includes the native-born children of immigrants, who occupied a demographic, sociological, and cultural middle ground. These children, though born in America and therefore automatically citizens of the United States, typically grew up in families torn between maintaining ethnic, national, and religious traditions and demonstrating their worthiness as new Americans. Their children were often their guide. The high percentage of foreigners in their midst led urban reformers to focus their efforts on immigrant children, who came to symbolize simultaneously all the new hopes for childhood and the new fears about immigration. In addition to the conflicts over acculturation that all immigrants faced, immigrant families with children also had to contend with important developments in thinking about children and childhood in general.

The Chaskes family, Jews from Hungary, had this studio photograph taken in 1922, several years after immigration. *(Courtesy of Jay Chaskes)*

The Emergence of a Protected Youth

Although less immediately visible than the changes wrought by mass immigration, changing attitudes toward children also were shaping American society and culture. During the earliest years of European settlement in British North America, Protestant colonists had seen children as dangerous, perhaps even depraved beings whose spirit must be broken to ensure a lifetime of godly service. Farm families operated as units, with even very young children contributing to the household economies. Children wore smaller versions of adult clothing and were generally viewed as quantitatively but not qualitatively different from their elders. Only the wealthiest elites could afford to treat their children differently, but they nonetheless saw them as miniature adults in everything but legal and possibly religious status. The American Revolution's rhetoric of overthrowing the patriarchal authority of England may have loosened the strictures of patriarchal household authority, but fathers still retained control of their families.

The nineteenth century brought a number of important changes to ideas about childhood and youth. Demographic shifts in the early 1800s resulted in smaller families with fewer children. Mothers gained considerably more familial power as fathers moved from the home to the industrial workplace. Changes in American Protestantism softened theological positions on infant damnation so that a new innocence became attached to an idealized childhood. The widespread growth of public education, beginning in the 1830s, helped draw a sharp boundary between childhood and adulthood for many white children. Along with formal education came a newly defined dependency of nonproductive children on their parents. These new ideas about childhood were related to other intellectual currents of mid- to late-nineteenth-century life, particularly evolutionary theory, with its focus on biology, environment, and stages of development. Children were now seen as qualitatively different from adults, progressing through stages of life with their own developmental and behavioral benchmarks. By the 1880s children were more typically seen as emotional investments than as economic assets.

As ideas about childhood as a distinct, ideally innocent and dependent stage of life took hold, an identifiable middle class formed around these conceptions. The home became a protected environment where fathers provided for their children, mothers sheltered and cared for them, and both parents inculcated them with moral values. Distinctions between boys and girls began at younger and younger ages, visible in different clothing and toys. Once childhood became so separate from adulthood, it also became necessary to conceive of adolescence as an essential stage of transition. Adolescence was a far more amorphous phase of development than childhood, as adolescents had intellectual and sexual similarities to adults, and often worked at jobs too. The idea of an intermediate developmental stage appealed broadly both to theorists who practiced the new social sciences of psychology and sociology and to Americans who increasingly attached adulthood to marriage and householding responsibilities rather than employment alone. Secondary schooling gradually filled in the gap as the idea of high school education spread among middle-class Americans. Even though most American families could not and did not embody the middle-class ideal of childhood and adolescence, the dominance of the model nonetheless exerted enormous influence across class, ethnic, and racial lines.

The inability of many—in some times and places, most—American families to follow this developmental model of childhood led to the prominence of children as objects first of charity, then of scientific philanthropy, and ultimately of social work. Mid-nineteenth century institutions promised to raise and discipline orphaned, abused, neglected, poor, and delinquent children if their parents could not or would not care for them. The child-saving movement at the turn of the century sought to counter the damages of rampant industrialization and capitalism to children's lives. Progressive reformers used the rhetoric of "a right to childhood" to argue that the state had a compelling interest in securing childhood for all children. Reform movements accepted without question the presumption that children were different from adults. They used that belief as a basis for the establishment of compulsory education, juvenile justice, and child-labor laws aimed at children as a distinct legal category. The legal basis of childhood operated on local, state, and national levels. For instance, from the 1880s through the 1920s, all states raised the age of consent from ten-to-twelve years old to sixteen-to-eighteen years old. The federal government showed its interest in children by convening the White House Conference on Dependent Children in 1909 and establishing the Children's Bureau in 1912. As with many other reform efforts, there was a significant transatlantic cast to the child-saving movement. In 1924 the League of Nations adopted the Declaration of the Rights of the Child. Even though the United States never joined the League, it firmly acknowledged the right to childhood. The best interests of children had become increasingly important. Yet immigrant families frequently held on to their own ideas about how to define the best interests of their own children.

Immigration and the American Social Mosaic

Although there has been continuous migration to the United States throughout its history, two major waves of immigration occurred before the passage of major restrictive legislation in the mid-1920s. The "first wave" of the 1840s and 1850s consisted primarily of immigrants from central and western Europe, with especially large numbers of Irish and German migrants. This wave also included sizable groups of Scandinavian and Chinese immigrants. Irish and Chinese laborers built much of the great railroad system that opened up the United States' share of the continent, allowing important numbers of immigrants to claim land and establish farms and small rural communities. Most of the first-wave immigrants stayed in the coastal cities that served as their ports of entry. New York, Baltimore, Boston, Philadelphia, and San Francisco grew rapidly as a result. Both secondary manufacturing centers like Providence and railroad hubs like Chicago also saw major influxes of immigrants. Native-born Americans viewed the foreigners with ambivalence and were particularly disturbed by the Catholicism of the Irish and many of the Germans. Nativist political parties sprang up, and violence was directed at Chinese laborers and Irish Catholics. By 1860, however, the great debates over slavery and ultimately the upheaval leading to the Civil War reduced immigration sharply.

Following the Civil War and the uneasy but eventually stable period of Reconstruction, a "second wave" of immigration to the United States began in the 1880s and lasted until the mid-1920s. The mass influx of immigrants was part of a worldwide population movement that began during the late nineteenth century, with millions of migrants from Europe and Asia heading to Canada, South America, and Australia, though the majority set out for the United States. They were motivated by both "push" factors, which led to their decisions to leave their homelands, and "pull" factors, which influenced them to make America their destination of choice. Push factors varied by national origin and ethnic background. Eastern European Jews faced steadily rising, violent anti-Semitism from the 1880s onward that made their lives increasingly intolerable; Mexicans confronted political instability and violence in the wake of the Mexican Revolution. Lower crop prices, higher tax rates, significant changes in land distribution policy, natural disasters, and the impact of modernization on traditional ways of life encouraged immigrants from around the globe to resolve to make new lives for themselves elsewhere.

By far the most important pull factor in this wave of migration was industrialization. Huge advances in industry and technology were turning the United States into a dominant force on the global economic scene, requiring endless supplies of labor, more manpower than the native-born U.S. population could supply. The mythic allure of a democratic, free society, where anyone who worked hard could rise, was another crucial pull factor for people who wished to improve their own circumstances and guarantee their children better lives than they could hope for in the Old World. The realization of this ideal was less important to the millions of immigrants than its possibility.

Thus the turn of the century saw a major increase in the number of immigrants coming to America. Steamship travel furthered migration across both the Atlantic and the Pacific oceans while railroad travel made crossing the border from Canada and Mexico easier. During the 1870s, 2.8 million immigrants arrived, but in the 1880s more than 5.2 million came, and 8.8 million more came between 1900 and 1910 alone. The population of the United States, especially the foreign-born percentage of that population, swelled dramatically.

This second wave of immigration differed in many respects from the first. Unlike their predecessors, the largest groups among turn-of-the-century immigrants were southern and eastern Europeans, especially Italians and Jews, and Mexicans, Japanese, and French Canadians. Most of the new immigrants aimed to find industrial rather than agricultural employment. As a result, a higher percentage of second-wave immigrants flocked to and stayed in urban centers, which offered housing, employment, and mutual assistance opportunities. Because economic opportunity was the chief motive for so many immigrants, there was a fairly high rate of return migration for some groups, like Italian men, who left whenever the United States experienced one of its periodic economic downturns or when they had amassed sufficient earnings to take home to the families they had left behind. Still, many immigrants came in family groups and planned to stay permanently. The large numbers of Catholics and Jews among these new immigrants reawakened the nativism, anti-Semitism, and anti-Catholicism of the Protestant majority, including second- and third-generation descendants of first-wave immigrants.

Along with internal migration to U.S. cities, foreign immigration transformed the landscape of America. Big cities like New York, Philadelphia, and San Francisco grew bigger, and smaller cities like Detroit, Pittsburgh, and Seattle exploded as they industrialized. By 1910 New York, Chicago, Boston, Cleveland, Detroit, Newark, and other cities had foreign-born populations of more than 30 percent, and in many cases native-born populations of foreign or mixed parentage of more than 40 percent. There continued to be large rural populations of certain ethnic groups, such as Norwegians and Czechs, but the new wave of turn-of-the-century immigration was largely urban in nature.

Cities offered benefits to immigrants beyond industrial opportunities. Large numbers of migrants from certain national or ethnic backgrounds led to clustering in both residential communities and employment. Although they were never isolated from other ethnic groups, immigrants tended to live in urban enclaves. Neighborhoods like New York's heavily Jewish Lower East Side or Pittsburgh's Polish Hill created a comfort zone for immigrants who could speak their native languages there and buy ethnic food and clothing. Discrimination also played a role in ethnic enclaves. Few other groups were willing to live in Chinatowns, for example. Neapolitans, Genoese, and Sicilians, who had never thought of themselves as compatriots, now found that native-born Americans considered them all Italians, and they began to develop that identity in Little Italy neighborhoods in a number of cities.

The process of chain migration, whereby one family member brought over other family members, friends, and neighbors from the old country and helped them find jobs and places to live, contributed to employment clustering. In certain New England textile mills, for example, nearly all the employees were French Canadians who migrated for jobs they knew would be open to them thanks to the recommendations of relatives and former neighbors. Although most turn-of-the-century immigrants tended to find work as unskilled or semi-skilled laborers, chain migration also led to the predominance of certain ethnic groups in particular fields of work. Jews were heavily concentrated in the garment industry, Poles in steel production and meatpacking, and Mexicans in commercial agriculture.

Immigrants in industrial America faced difficulties at every turn. Urban housing was cramped and crowded; the private housing market could not cope with the thousands of new residents arriving daily. In most cities, immigrants paid high rents in multiple-family dwellings in neighborhoods of intense population density. Single buildings might contain several hundred people sharing the most minimal sanitary facilities. Tenement housing offered little light or air and often provided no running water or heat. The demand for living spaces near workplaces was so high that landlords built housing in every available space in the urban core. High rates of illness and death resulted from these filthy, crowded living conditions. Forms of urban housing varied from city to city, but problems of population density, disease, and attendant crime appeared everywhere. Minimal privacy obtained in such circumstances as families took in relatives and boarders to make ends meet. With no space to do anything but eat, sleep, and perhaps work at home, immigrants spilled out of the tenements and onto the city streets.

For the new immigrants, work conditions were no better. Poorly regulated factories crowded workers into unsuitable spaces and demanded continuous labor in dangerous conditions. Employees injured on the job had no safety net of public services and no legal recourse. Workers labored long days and nights in unskilled jobs with little opportunity for advancement. Accidents occurred often; fires broke out regularly. With the enormous numbers of immigrants entering the United States, workers realized they were easily replaceable. As a result of these conditions, for most urban immigrants work offered hardly any respite from the discomforts and dangers of home life.

Rural immigrants dealt with challenges peculiar to their situation. The growth of commercial agriculture, particularly on the West Coast where many Mexican and Japanese immigrants settled, meant that they were far more likely to work for others than to establish their own farms or businesses. Their work was agricultural rather than industrial but was nonetheless seasonal wage labor. Rural housing was rudimentary at best. Even those immigrant farmers who managed to stake claims and build farms in the Midwest were likely to invest more of their resources in barns and farm equipment than in their own houses. Agricultural laborers lived in shacks or tents even more exposed to the elements than tenements and equally lacking in sanitary facilities.

Progressive reformers responded to housing and health concerns thrown into such sharp relief by turn-of-the-century immigration by pushing for tighter building codes and building model tenements. Municipal engineers made real progress in developing city services. Improved sewage and waste-disposal systems, water purification, and fire prevention enhanced the living conditions of all city dwellers. Public health officials used advances in medical knowledge of disease and its origins to promote personal hygiene and proper diet. Many cities opened clean milk depots and health clinics. These reform efforts gradually raised the standards of urban living, though public facilities never reached all urban dwellers and had little impact on rural populations. And no matter how well intentioned they were, reformers came into constant class and cultural conflict with the immigrants they were trying to help.

In both rural and urban settings, immigrants maintained at least some cultural continuity through family traditions and the establishment of religious and communal institutions. Ethnic institutions like newspapers, saloons, and churches helped ease the difficult adjustment to a new life. This was particularly important given the abject poverty in which most immigrants lived at least temporarily. They faced intense nativism from Americans who disdained and feared all non-Protestant and racially distinct newcomers and wavered between demanding instant assimilation or contending that Americanization was neither possible nor desirable for such inferior peoples. Given these intense challenges, immigrants relied on one another for support amid their difficult lives and their uncertainty about whether they had made the best decisions for themselves and their children. Their problems became central concerns of the Progressive Era.

A Clash of Cultures

The widespread reform efforts of the Progressive Era spurred an awakening social conscience among many middle-class Americans and led to greater government responsibility as well as interference in daily life. But those who reflexively resisted change, and especially those who blamed mass migration for the unwelcome changes the modern world was introducing into their lives, resented the reforms. Organized labor, for instance, structured in the American Federation of Labor by craft and skill, refused to expand to include millions of unskilled immigrant workers, fearing job competition and lower wages. Labor leaders also worried, with some justification, that the various ethnic groups would not cooperate with one another on the job. Rural and small-town American Protestants, many of whom already viewed urban life with great suspicion, blamed immigrants for populating cities with teeming hordes of unruly, non-English-speaking, licentious Papists and Jews. They aimed a special hostility at those immigrants, like Japanese and Mexicans, who were perceived as racially distinct. Many native-born Americans were not interested in noting the points of similarity between themselves and the new immigrants. In fact they shared ideas about the importance of job advancement and property ownership, but the difference in cultural values took center stage. The result was twofold: a strong Americanization movement that insisted on total assimilation as the price immigrants must pay for entering American life, and a powerful nativist movement that campaigned for restrictive immigration laws to close the doors of America to the foreign element.

The public and collective culture of working-class life seemed both distasteful and undesirable to even the most sympathetic middle-class observers. Whether they were immigrants, African Americans, or any other members of the working class, poor families functioned very differently from financially secure ones.

Working-class families operated as economic units, with individual family members expected to subjugate their own desires to the needs of the household. This collective structure responded to the reality that a single income could not sustain a working-class family. Unskilled labor paid so poorly that only the very rare, very fortunate married man with children could provide for his household with his wages alone. The labor of other household members was necessary; when no adult male was present or gainfully employed, the need was even greater. In immigrant families, children usually made up the economic gap. Women contributed as well by taking in boarders and performing some kind of work at home.

The American middle-class model, in sharp contrast, posited homes as domestic havens where family members were free to pursue their individual interests. The ideal middle-class man earned a steady salary in a work environment removed from the home and provided for his wife and children's every material need. The ideal middle-class woman cared for the home and provided emotional and domestic support to her husband and children. The ideal middle-class children enjoyed safe and secure childhoods with ample time for education, play, and moral development. Recreation was fairly private in nature and took place in the home, which was central to every aspect of family life.

Clearly it was unrealistic for most immigrants to follow this model, though many did aspire to it as the ultimate proof of eventual financial security and acculturation. Working-class households might well include nuclear families, but they were also likely to include additional relatives and boarders. Family privacy could not be a priority. With no recreational space available at home, working-class immigrants and others participated in the development of the public culture of commercial entertainment. Thus amusement parks, dance halls, and movie theaters became major instruments of Americanization even as they served a public purpose far removed from middle-class ideas about tasteful and appropriate leisure activity.

Some points of contact between middle- and working-class life could be found, including consumerism and public education. Although most immigrants had literally no money to spare when they first arrived in the United States, as soon as they could afford to do so they began to purchase the goods that marked their new country as a nation of abundance. Buying consumer products ranging from fashionable hats to brand-name grocery items demonstrated immigrants' success and their interest in adopting the material culture of American life. Across class boundaries, turn-of-the-century Americans participated in the creation of a peculiarly American consumer culture.

Public education shaped another space for cultural homogenization across class. Students, parents, teachers, and educational theorists noted and sometimes perpetuated class and racial distinctions, but the ideological commitment to free public schools nevertheless provided common experiences of both education and socialization. In urban areas, residential segregation along class and ethnic lines often resulted in schools with similarly distinct populations, but the growing standardization of curricula, especially on the elementary school level, yielded a fairly standard educational experience. Relatively few immigrants enjoyed the luxury of a high school education, but the very existence of free secondary schooling allowed for the possibility of an American adolescence modeled on middle-class stages of life.

When immigrants arrived in America, the widely accepted ideas they encountered about childhood, children, and adolescence seemed just as strange to most of them as new foods like bananas and new sports like baseball. They cared enormously about their children's physical well-being and moral development; many had migrated for the explicit purpose of offering their children better lives. But they were not used to or enthusiastic about state intervention in their traditional roles of family authority. For example, most immigrant parents did not believe that the state should or could force them to send their children to school. They demanded to know how their families could survive if their children studied rather than worked. This question, of course, was echoed by millions of working-class families of all backgrounds across America. Viewing children as individuals and emotional investments rather than as part of a collective family economic enterprise was a luxury of the middle and upper classes, who did not worry constantly about putting bread on the table. Native-born working-class families shared this grievance yet typically aspired to achieve the middle-class model of family structure and childhood. Immigrant parents, bewildered and even repulsed by some American social norms, often set their sights on different goals, more in keeping with their own cultural traditions.

Their children, however, grew up exposed to both sets of ideas and understandably gravitated toward the vision of protected childhood that would allow them both to maximize their potential and to do so as individual Americans. Immigrant children rarely set out to hurt their parents, but they found that their best chance for achieving success and recognition—even pleasure—during their childhood and adolescence lay in acculturating to mainstream American ideals. Although economic necessity often interfered with their attempts to live out their own version of the American dream, ideas about childhood and youth became one more dividing line between the immigrant parents and children who made up such a large part of turn-of-the-century America.

CHAPTER TWO

The Landscape of Early Childhood

As we stop in front of a tenement . . . a dirty baby in a single brief garment—yet a sweet, human little baby despite its dirt and tatters—tumbles off the lowest step, rolls over once, clutches my leg with an unconscious grip, and goes to sleep on the flagstones, its curly head pillowed on my boot.

—Jacob Riis, *How the Other Half Lives* (1890)[1]

OF ALL the wretched sights greeting Jacob Riis as he made his way through the teeming tenements of Lower New York in 1887 and 1888, none appalled him as much as the wretched babies. There were babies swathed in dirty rags, lying on doorsills, and recognizable as living creatures only by their faint wailing. There were babies suspended from low ceilings in makeshift hammocks to keep them out of the way of family sweatshops. There were abandoned babies in rows of cradles in foundling homes, too sick to cry or eat or live. There were babies whose unclaimed bodies appeared each spring in the river. There were babies clutched in their mothers' arms whose sunken eyes seemed to Riis helpless and hopeless. And there were babies who turned out to be nothing but bundles of cloth artfully arranged around an ear of corn or a block of wood, proffered to the stranger on the street as justification for begging. As Riis and his "raiding party" of photographers picked their way through the crowded city streets, intent on revealing the misery therein, babies everywhere revealed to them the horrific conditions of the urban poor. Nearly all these infants were immigrant children.

As Riis discovered early during the period of late-nineteenth- and early-twentieth-century reform that became known as the Progressive Era, the suffering of children was sure to elicit adult response. A titillated middle- and upper-class audience might gasp in mingled horror and delight at the sight of drunken tramps and starving seamstresses, first at a viewing of Riis's traveling magic lantern slide shows and then in the published version of *How the Other Half Lives*. Yet disturbing images of homeless little boys and tubercular little girls were far more likely than images of broken-down adults to move the privileged classes to action. Children, especially young white children, seemed both the most pitiable and the most salvageable. What mother could gaze upon such heartbreak and neglect and not donate money or time to saving the children who lived so close to and yet so far from her own? What father could count the costs of disease and crime and not act to impose social order? Indeed, what American could fail to seize the opportunity to save these children by assuaging their hunger, uplifting their spirits, and transforming them into proper American children, well tended, well schooled, and well behaved? If immigrant parents could not take care of their own children, never mind their excuses of poverty and hardship and lack of opportunity, American parents and teachers and reformers and doctors and nurses and social workers would have to step in. Riis understood that deploying children as symbols of all that was wrong would be the most effective strategy for making things right.

When Riis first published *How the Other Half Lives* in 1890, the "second wave" of mass migration to the United States had been under way for approximately a decade. In the years that followed, immigrants from around the globe poured into American cities, which were completely unprepared to deal with the influx. Many immigrants initially came alone but eventually sent for their families or started families in their new homes. As a result, the face of immigration in America belonged not only to the industrial worker or the farmer but also to the children either born in the United States or brought over at a young age. The foreign-born population in some cities climbed to more than 50 percent, and the number of children born in America to foreign-born parents in effect elevated the number of immigrants higher still. Americans, alarmed by the waves of migration from such "undesirable" locales as southern and eastern Europe, Mexico, and Japan, viewed the proliferation of immigrant infants and toddlers as harbingers of doom for so-called American values and mores. At the same time immigrant parents viewed their children as the natural benefactors of the risk of starting over in a new land. The frail shoulders of young immigrant children carried the double burden of their new countrymen's fears and their parents' expectations.

Changes in ideas about childhood during the nineteenth century contributed to the ways in which very young immigrant children were perceived. By the mid-nineteenth century, relatively few Americans still believed that infants were born damned and required severe moral instruction if they were to be saved. Instead, particularly among the expanding and increasingly influential middle class, babies became the embodiment of a new innocence of youth. Families strove to provide healthy, nurturing environments for young children that would encourage their sense of wonder and discovery. Ironically, some of these same middle-class parents failed to translate their nascent understanding of environmental influences to their immigrant counterparts, blaming nature rather than nurture for the social ills of immigrant children. Yet the idea of infant innocence was so powerful by 1890 that, as Riis found, the sight of needy babies moved the hearts of observers as adults in similarly desperate straits did not. With the gradual emergence of a scientific approach to childhood during the first decades of the twentieth century came the conviction that philanthropists and, later, social workers could do a great service for immigrant babies through health care and educational programs and institutions. Not coincidentally, such efforts, whether carried out by church volunteers, visiting nurses, or settlement house workers, would necessarily also improve the overall tenor of American life by standardizing infant care according to the best scientific approach.

The professional agents of social change, who undoubtedly cared about the well-being of immigrant babies even as they ran roughshod over immigrant parents, did not count on resistance, but that was what they found. Immigrant parents, it turned out, had their own ideas about early childhood. Mothers typically retained traditional birthing practices, and families celebrated new arrivals with customs that reinforced their differences from mainstream American culture. Ethnic communities took note of the naked hostility aimed their way by eugenicists, who condemned white Anglo-Saxon Protestants for committing race suicide by allowing immigrant parents to surpass their procreative efforts. Reformers sometimes rejected vicious rhetoric but still redoubled their efforts to turn immigrant babies into good American children and hence American adults. The kindergarten movement was a major expression of the desire to use young children to shift the loyalties of ethnic communities.

Despite their ambivalence on other matters, many immigrant parents also embraced this goal and took advantage of all the reform efforts that seemed to promise their children a better life. Their economic status might not have allowed their children the luxury of a protected infancy and innocent youth, but they nonetheless aspired to demonstrate their success in America by raising American children. In addition, despite the vitriol aimed at them, all children of

foreign parents who were born in the United States were automatically citizens. They would not just disappear from public consideration or participation. In both a symbolic and a real sense,
immigrant babies embodied hope for families, communities, and
reformers alike.

Born Between Two Worlds

Immigrant infants began life in a world with preconceived ideas
about their identities. Legal doctrine determined their citizenship
status, but even a legally defined status could not protect them from
critics who saw their very existence as a shadow falling on the racial
character of the nation. Their earliest experiences were primarily
shaped by their parents, whose concerns about preserving ethnic
traditions tended to appear most strongly at times of celebration
and crisis, both characteristic of childbirth. One aspect of identity
that provided some area of agreement for family, community, and
outside observers was gender. Across ethnic groups and class divides, the fact of being a boy or a girl played an important role in
shaping the early childhood of immigrants. Ultimately all immigrant children were born into families with particular worldviews
and traditions. All were born into specific living conditions that influenced their earliest years. And all were seen by both their families
and outside observers as symbols as well as real children. Whether
born abroad and brought to the United States or born in the new
country, infants and young children participated, through their
families, in all the issues surrounding the complex processes of immigration and acculturation.

Citizenship. Even the youngest immigrant children's identities
were subject, in part, to preordained categories, apart from their individual circumstances. In the United States there were three possi-

ble bases for immigrant classification. U.S. census records generally used people's country of origin or their mother tongue, but the Bureau of Immigration relied on their racial identity. Immigrant children born in the United States or to U.S. citizens abroad were automatically citizens, a legal identity with tremendous implications for themselves and their families. But despite the relatively liberal nature of this policy, there were exceptions and exclusions throughout the period of mass migration from approximately 1880 to 1924. At times the legal status of immigrant children depended on the fluctuating distinctions between the doctrine of *jus sanguinus*, which connected children's citizenship to the status of their parents, no matter where the parents were physically present, and *jus solis*, which connected children's citizenship to the place their parents were physically present at the time of their children's birth, regardless of the parents' citizenship status. Children who immigrated to the United States at a young age, particularly after 1900, were likely to become citizens even when their parents did not. Immigrant children born in the United States generally qualified for citizenship according to *jus solis*. Due to discriminatory legislation, however, *jus sanguinus* sometimes prevailed for Asian children, meaning that they could be classified, like their parents, as aliens ineligible for citizenship.

Chinese and Japanese immigrants fought this discrimination so blatant in U.S. immigration law. Chinese Americans who had attained citizenship during the nineteenth century used their status to resist the Chinese Exclusion Act of 1882. They returned to the United States after visits to China and reported the births of "paper sons" who could later claim the right to be admitted to the United States based on their fathers' existing citizenship status. Virtually no one claimed a "paper daughter," as girls did not seem valuable enough to lie about. This loophole allowed thousands of Chinese men to come to the United States after 1882, despite exclusion. In 1907, for instance, California merchant Wong Hang Dong swore in an affidavit that he was a citizen of the United States when he visited China and fathered Wong Sun Fat, an eighteen-year-old boy then in China waiting for admission to the United States. The pictures of putative father and son attached to the affidavit did not prove paternity, but Sun Fat was allowed to immigrate. When a series of land laws in 1913, 1920, and 1923 made it illegal for aliens ineligible for citizenship to own land or even lease it, Japanese immigrants maneuvered around the law by putting land in their American-born children's names. Unlike Asian immigrants, European immigrants had greater access to citizenship for themselves, but their American-born children often achieved it first as a combination of birthright and accident of geography.

Many American observers of the growing number of immigrants expressed alarm at the sheer volume of new citizens the relatively liberal U.S. policy created. The dismay that native-born Americans felt at the sight of immigrant toddlers was just one part of the mixed reaction they had to immigrants in general. The overriding fear was one of miscegenation, which at the turn of the century referred to any kind of racial mixing, not just sexual relations between whites and African Americans. An opponent of Caucasian and Japanese intermarriage declared, "In that woman's arms is a baby. What is that baby? It isn't Japanese. It isn't white."[2] Children of what a 1905 California law termed miscegenation became the literal embodiment of border crossings, deeply threatening to those who believed in not only the natural existence but also the imperative separation of races.

Many Americans had long been willfully blind to the social, racial, and cultural mixing that has always been part of the U.S. history. They preferred to see their history, and as a result, their country, in purely black and white terms, with African Americans cast as the only racial "others" and all other groups rendered invisible. But after the turn of the century the wave of immigration from places where white Americans did not perceive the native populations as white, even if they were not quite black either, changed the terms of the debate over national character. A 1928 American Eugenics Society report, citing the high birthrate of Mexicans in the Southwest who had been born as U.S. citizens, commented, "This is not a question of pocketbook or of the 'need of labor' or of economics. It is a question of the character of future races."[3] T. J. Woofter, Jr.'s book *Race and Ethnic Groups in American Life* (1933) gloomily concluded that race suicide was inevitable, given the immigrant children of undesirable racial stock then swarming the nation.[4] Both these views were representative of their times. It was not surprising that groups and individuals already committed to the ideas of scientific racism should think about immigrant children in this light.

But more sympathetic observers used equally charged language in speaking of immigrant children. While blaming environment rather than heredity, the authors of a 1920 pamphlet in Los Angeles worried that "every time a baby dies the nation loses a prospective citizen, but in every slum child who lives, the nation has a probable consumptive and a possible criminal."[5] No racial hierarchy appeared explicitly in this comment, but given that the largest contingent of "slum children" in the city was Mexican, the specter of comparison between "white" and "foreign" children hung there unspoken. Even the most sensitive commentators, such as Emily Greene Balch, whose 1910 book *Our Slavic Fellow Citizens* implied in its title her welcoming attitude toward immigrants, paused when confronted with immigrant children. Balch explained, "However well one may think of the Pole, the New Englander may be pardoned a pang of regret. . . . It is with a rather rueful smile that he observes the swarms of funny little tots, with their tow heads bundled in kerchiefs."[6] This American observer seemed distressed not by labor competition or foreign languages or strange customs but rather by the mere presence of oddly dressed children that she acknowledged must change the nature of the country. Immigrant children carried the symbolic freight of native-born Americans' discomfort with foreignness in their midst.

New Life, Old Customs. This foreignness seemed apparent even in the case of infants and toddlers, as parents tended to maintain ethnic customs around childbirth and infancy longer than for almost any other occasion. This is hardly surprising given the fact that childbirth fell squarely into the domain of women, who may have worked outside the home but were also largely responsible for maintaining ethnic traditions inside it. Religion also played a role, as most immigrant groups practiced religious rituals related to childbirth and were unlikely to forgo them even if they were not always in other ways devout. Performing a circumcision on a Jewish boy or baptizing a Mexican girl was their parents' way of setting them on the right path.

Immigrant children born in America entered the worlds of their families and communities literally as well as figuratively. As late as the 1920s, approximately 21,000 of 58,000 births a year in Chicago took place at home rather than in a hospital.[7] The percentage of immigrant home births remained significantly higher, though some groups of women, such as Jews, adopted hospital childbirth before others, such as Italians. Physicians rarely attended these home births, and immigrant women usually received no formal pre- or postnatal care. Describing his new daughter's birth to his parents back home in Denmark, Valdemar Wahl wrote in 1883, "I didn't have anything to do with it, thank God. I could hardly have delivered her before Mr. Esquire and his wife came flying in and did it. His wife really knew what she was doing."[8] In the rural Scandinavian communities of the Upper Midwestern prairies, neighboring women were the only ones available to help others through labor and delivery, if they could get there on time. During the blizzard of 1888, Olive Dahl's mother gave birth to her alone in a North

Dakota farmhouse when Olive's father could not return with help before the delivery. Less isolated women, too, relied on neighbors, as did Albertina di Grazia's mother, who delivered all eight of her children at home in Scotch Plains, New Jersey.

Most immigrant children were born with the help of midwives, who were present nearly everywhere immigrants settled. In 1916 in a Polish community in central Wisconsin, midwives attended more than 60 percent of the deliveries. Children delivered by midwives actually boasted a lower mortality rate than those brought into the world by doctors.[9] The midwives might be professionals within the ethnic community or just neighbors who served as needed. In Japanese communities a *sanba*, a professional trained in modern midwifery in Japan, delivered most of the babies known as the Nisei generation. *Sanbas* took great pride in their professional status and combined their medical knowledge with the traditions of Japanese childbirth. When a *sanba* was called in, she brought her patient a *hara obi*, a cotton sash that pregnant women wrapped around their abdomens after they first felt fetal movement. The *hara obi* provided back support and traditionally brought good luck. *Sanbas* maintained other Japanese birthing customs as well, such as silent deliveries and the traditional—if elusive for working women— twenty-one-day period of rest following childbirth. Although *sanbas* focused their efforts on Japanese women, in California they also delivered Mexican babies and served as bridges between ethnic communities that literally had no language in common other than childbirth.

Even after the medical model of childbirth began to make headway among white middle-class Americans, immigrants usually avoided hospitals, due to either poverty or mistrust. When Mary Paik's mother gave birth in a Sacramento boardinghouse, the baby almost died. Rather than take the newborn to the hospital or even call a doctor, Mary and her father saved the baby by massaging and bathing him according to traditional Korean methods. They were unwilling to turn over one of their own to strangers, even professional strangers in a position to help.

While immigrant women naturally relied on their families and on one another for labor and delivery, they could count on no one else for help once the baby was born. Japanese women typically worked until just before labor and took minimal time to recover before returning to work. Emma Duke, a social investigator who studied immigrant children in Johnstown, Pennsylvania, in 1913, noted of one Polish woman:

> At 5 o'clock Monday evening went to sister's to return washboard, having just finished day's washing. Baby born while there; sister too young to assist in any way; woman not accustomed to midwife anyway, so she cut cord herself; washed baby at sister's house, walked home, cooked supper for boarders, and was in bed by 8 o'clock. Got up and ironed next day and day following; it tired her, so she then stayed in bed two days.

Infants were women's responsibility, just like domestic work. No one else could or would take on this work, so women usually could not allow childbirth to distract them for long. Observers like Duke, who for all her attempted objectivity could not hide either the admiration or the distress she felt for the anonymous Polish woman who grew tired, concluded that immigrant families saw the business of childbirth as no one's but their own. When women delivered with the help of neighbors, they sometimes did not even bother to obtain birth certificates for their children. In order to conduct her study of all the children born in Johnstown in 1911, Duke had to comb through church records and make home visits to identify them.[10] This disinterest in obtaining official recognition of their babies may have signified some immigrant parents' symbolic assertion of control over their children's future, a control they probably realized might be hard to come by in their new land.

Just as childbirth took place largely within the purview of the community, so did the various celebrations and ceremonies of childhood that were typical of all immigrant groups. When a baby was born to one of the Germans from Russia living on the Nebraska plains, neighbors would bring the mother noodle soup for strength. Mexican women relied on their neighbors to bring them the appropriate "hot" foods, such as milk, tortillas, broth, and meat; "cold" foods like pork, fruit, beans, and vegetables might threaten breastfeeding. As soon as a boy was born to Japanese parents, neighbors came to offer their congratulations, bringing the fertility symbols of eggs or fish for the mother and blankets for the baby. A hundred days after a birth, Japanese parents who practiced Shinto would go to a shrine for a ceremony. Kentaro Takatsui was born in Mukilteo, Washington, but his family traveled to the Shinto shrine in Seattle for the event. Traditional Chinese mothers did not leave their homes for a month after childbirth, but even if household economics did not allow for such a break, parties held in homes for new babies included red eggs for happiness and pickled ginger for long life. These parties were followed by "full month" celebrations one month after the babies were born.

Christian immigrants also celebrated births in church settings, with Mexican *bautismo* ceremonies followed by fiestas. Bruna Pieracci recalled riding the train from the mining town where she grew up to the nearest Catholic church each time her mother had a baby. Each baptism was followed by a group photograph to commemorate the holy day. Many Greek and Russian Orthodox families maintained the custom of churching, with new mothers going to church for a purification ritual four to six weeks after childbirth. Feasts for friends, family, and neighbors usually followed. While most of these traditions demonstrated cultural persistence in a new land, there were also signs of acculturation within celebrations of childbirth. By the early twentieth century the Chinese community in San Francisco began to hold baby showers, a sign of adopting the consumer ethos and American customs surrounding childbirth. A few Jewish families even chose physicians rather than religious functionaries to perform circumcisions on their sons.

Naming practices clearly indicated the balance that many immigrant parents tried to strike for their children between preserving heritage and adopting American norms. Pardee Lowe's parents gave their children both Chinese names based on family heritage and English names based on notable figures they admired. Thus Pardee was named after the governor of California, and his sisters were named after the wives of presidents. His twin brothers' names, Woodrow Wilson Lowe and Thomas Riley Marshall Lowe, were so unusual that the media reported their christening in a Chinese Christian church. The Lowe children always used their English names and were greatly discomfited when someone addressed them by their Chinese names. Gender played a role in naming practices as well. The Beppu family of Seattle gave their daughter the Japanese name of Hiro but named their sons Grant, Lincoln, Monroe, and Taft, after former American presidents.

Other immigrant parents found different kinds of compromises. Frederick Bergman, writing to his sister back home in Sweden, noted that his daughter was christened Hildegard, an old family name, but was called Ruth in their Austin, Texas, community. Many Polish families tried to keep Polish names alive, but even if they chose names more readily accepted in the larger American society, they honored their heritage by celebrating name days. All the boys named Joseph, for example, celebrated St. Joseph's day as their name day rather than celebrating their individual birthdays. Greek children were often named after the saint of the day on which they were born.

Immigrant parents knew the symbolic value of naming their children, and so did church and state bureaucracies. Male immigrants from India who married Mexican women set up households in the Southwest where the Catholic church insisted their children be baptized with Catholic or Spanish rather than Punjabi names.

New York City bureaucrats were notorious for giving parents a hard time if they chose names deemed too difficult to pronounce or just too foreign. In one case a parish priest had to intervene with the health department after an official thought that "Lucia" was a boy's name and filled out the birth certificate incorrectly for the new daughter of Italian parents. Religious or state institutions could not really control immigrants' naming practices, but they staked their own claim to immigrant children's lives by trying to impose their standards onto parent-child relationships.

Boys and Girls. One area of agreement for most Americans during the late nineteenth and early twentieth centuries was that of role division by gender. Immigrants might welcome daughters with as much enthusiasm as sons, particularly if there were already a boy in the family, but no one expected boys and girls to live similar lives. Differences in treatment began early. In 1880 neither traditional ethnic garb nor American layettes made much distinction between baby boys' and girls' dress, but by 1920 the color coding of blue for boys and pink for girls had crossed cultural divides and become relatively pervasive. Studies carried out by reformers found that parents—mothers as well as fathers—typically gave boys more to eat than girls. Less crying was tolerated from infant girls than from infant boys. Parents extended more independence of movement to their sons than to their daughters.

Certain cultures upheld very different attitudes toward boys and girls. A poem from the Chinese *Book of Songs* expressed the traditional distinctions:

> *So he begets a son*
> *And puts him to sleep upon a bed*
> *Clothes him in robes*
> *Gives him a jade sceptre to play with*
> *The child's howling is very lusty*
> *In red greaves shall he flare*

Be lord and king of house and home
Then he bears a daughter
And puts her upon the ground
Clothes her in swaddling clothes
Gives her a loom-whorl to play with
For her no decorations, no emblems
Her only care, the wine and food
And how to give no trouble to father and mother[11]

In this culture, as in others, the expectations for boys and girls differed enormously. The son received more elaborate clothing and toys than the daughter. The volume of his cries was perceived as a sign of his strength where the daughter's silence was a virtue. The son could look forward to becoming a head of his own household some day; the daughter's main goal was to tend to her parents' needs. Clearly this poem represents an exaggerated vision of the relative value of boys and girls. Plenty of immigrant parents loved and cherished their daughters and tried their hardest to give them as much as they could. But there is no denying the impact of such gender distinctions on children's real lives. Immigrant girls' memoirs often recalled, with barely disguised hurt, the privileges their brothers received just for being boys. Immigrant boys' memoirs, too, noted the different treatment in passing, though understandably with less regret. Life was not necessarily easier for young boys than young girls, but since most immigrant families and cultures were patriarchal in nature, there were natural advantages for even the youngest men.

Early Challenges

Gender may have played a part in shaping children's early experiences, but for most the economic struggles of their immigrant families played an even larger role. The constant, grinding struggle to make a living occupied every member of most immigrant families, even the youngest. In households where the family was the economic unit, children became contributors very early in life. Even before they began to earn money themselves, they accompanied their parents and older siblings to their places of work. Although their presence in factories and fields scandalized observers, they were probably no worse off there than at home, where living conditions were generally wretched. Young immigrant children of all backgrounds ran a continual risk of illness and death. The infant mortality rate was shockingly high throughout the period of mass migration—nearly 20 percent of children died before reaching five years of age—though by 1920 it began to decline. On this score immigrant children were not so different from their counterparts in native-born families. Working-class people in turn-of-the-century America, whether African Americans, eighth-generation Southerners, or recently arrived French Canadians, suffered from malnutrition, disease, and all the other accoutrements of poverty. Progressive reformers worked to combat these conditions, and immigrant families tried to maximize what they had, but the deplorable circumstances of both urban and rural working-class life called for a steep upward battle. The birth-control movement appealed to numerous immigrant groups looking for strategies to improve the health of both mothers and children and to limit the number of mouths to feed.

Toddling to Work. One of the characteristics of immigrant families that outside observers found most disturbing was the presence of very young immigrant children in the workplace. In turn-of-the-century Hawaii, for instance, all Japanese and Korean adults had to work to sustain their households. Women took infants and toddlers with them to the fields and left them on mats or in boxes nearby. Describing Polish onion farmers in Massachusetts, *Outlook*

Although immigrants were less likely to settle in the Deep South than in other regions of the country, they went wherever they could find work—as in this shrimp company in Biloxi, Mississippi, in 1911. Note the numerous children in the photo. *(Library of Congress)*

magazine reported in 1910 that "the children first inspect the onions from their baby carriages . . . the baby handles his own bottle, which sours in the sun, learning self-reliance young."[12] Mexican family labor depended on young children to watch the babies as well as help with agricultural tasks. Parents marveled at their own children's adaptability. One farm worker recalled, "At the end of the day my wife and I would be ready to drop of weariness, but the children had to be called from chasing fireflies at bedtime."[13] The absence of a traditional extended family, including grandparents and other relatives, made it especially difficult for many immigrants to rear their children in a protected environment.

    The horror expressed by social workers and educators about these very young workers took on special urgency when immigrant children were involved, but in fact these patterns could be found in

When families hired themselves out for agricultural labor, they preferred to work among others of similar ethnic background for ease of communication. Here a six-year-old Syrian boy and his eight-year-old sister work in a cranberry bog in Massachusetts, in 1911. *(Library of Congress)*

many native-born working-class families. Young children in mill families went to work with their parents as often in Southern white families in North Carolina as in French-Canadian families in Maine. The idealized middle-class family dependent on the father's living wage was as far removed from most native-born children as from immigrant children, but to many observers the gap between these idealized values and immigrants' experiences seemed wider. In reality the cycle of work functioned in similar ways for most poor families. Women's work depended on the number of children they had, how many were old enough to work or possibly to go to school, and the availability of some form of child care. Across ethnic backgrounds, married women with small children often tried to work from home, either by taking in boarders or by such work as sewing artificial flowers or making matchboxes. Very few could afford to abstain from income-producing labor for any length of time. For immigrant families as for other working-class families, a pattern of child labor as well as women's labor resulted from economic necessity. Chinese children, for instance, worked from a very young age. Toddlers might accompany their mothers to factories, slightly older children might fold clothes in laundries, and adolescents might prepare food at restaurants. Although the nature of their work changed as they grew older and more adept, immigrant children typically began to work from the earliest ages.

Health and Living Conditions. The physical environments of most young immigrant children were almost universally miserable. Immigrant families in cities commonly lived in crowded, noisy, dirty tenements arranged for maximum sleeping room. Parents, children, and boarders crowded together in apartments below street level. Their tenements faced the sewage that moved through rear alleys. The Scorzofa family, which included both parents and several children, lived with seven boarders in four rooms on the third floor of a frame house in Pittsburgh. Without plumbing in the house, they depended on the hydrant in the yard for water. The street was muddy, unpaved, and often flooded.

The very walls of tenements teemed with bugs and bacteria. In a 1903 report on "The Lung Block," an area of New York's Lower East Side notorious for incubating tuberculosis, the settlement worker Ernest Poole observed that "the Plague lives in darkness and filth—filth in halls, over walls and floors, in sinks and closets . . . rooms here have held death ready and waiting for years." With no access to water, sunlight, or fresh air, tenement dwellers fell victim to contagious diseases from the earliest ages. As Poole wrote of the toddlers in the neighborhood, "at the age of two they are found alone in the street, already imbibing its deep muddy wisdom."[14]

Mexican migrant families lived in temporary shacks that provided little shelter from the elements. This one in Tempe, Arizona, circa 1894, had an outdoor oven. *(Smithsonian Institution National Anthropological Archives, courtesy of Arizona State University Library)*

Even parents' best efforts to keep their children clean by taking them to public bathhouses, as Pardee Lowe's mother did in San Francisco's Chinatown, failed to overcome the unwholesome environment so dangerous to small children.

Infants and toddlers in rural areas fared somewhat better in their access to fresh air. Still, their living conditions too were grim. An 1895 study of Mexicans in New Mexico reported that large families usually lived in small, windowless single rooms with one door and minimal light. They had no flooring other than the packed earth, and the flat adobe roofs provided only scant protection against the elements. Groups of families in these dwellings shared easily contaminated wells for water. Farms on the Great Plains were equally unlikely to have running water and brought children into constant contact with frequently diseased animals, though they too provided fresh air that urban tenements could not. Tuberculosis appeared much less often among rural children than among urban children, but tuberculosis was scarcely the only threat to children's health.

Infant mortality was consistently high within immigrant communities of all backgrounds and geographic locations. In 1880 the mortality rate in Lowell, Massachusetts's Little Canada section was 29.6 babies per 1,000. Fifty percent of French-Canadian deaths were children under the age of five.[15] When visiting poor immigrants in Philadelphia during the late nineteenth century, the agents of the Home Missionary Society recorded a startling number of entries noting "lost a child."[16] In 1900 about a third of Polish and Italian women saw a child die within one year of birth.[17] From 1900 to 1925 in the farming community of Sunderland, Massachusetts, the Polish community had a 17 percent infant mortality rate compared to 7 percent among the native born.[18] A 1920 chart listing the infant mortality rates per 1,000 births showed that compared to the native-born mothers' loss rate of 75.8, Polish mothers lost 121.8, Austrian mothers lost 112.9, Canadian mothers lost 99.3, Hungarian mothers lost 93.7, and Irish mothers lost 90.7. Only Scandinavian mothers lost fewer infants (66.4) than American-born mothers, possibly because Scandinavian families tended to live in rural rather than urban areas.[19] Tuberculosis, diphtheria, and measles were among the leading killers of infants under one year of age, though gastrointestinal, respiratory, and infectious diseases also struck immigrant homes, wherever they were. The only preventive medicines were smallpox vaccinations and diphtheria antitoxins, neither widely available to populations that could not afford to pay for health care.

When immigration laws were tightened from time to time after 1900, in an effort to prevent children who already had diseases from entering the United States, immigrant children with trachoma and other illnesses were deported back to their points of embarkation. If a young child was deported due to a health problem, an adult usually had to go too, which broke up family groups. The rejection rate at Ellis Island was only about 1 percent, but at Angel Island, the point of entry for most Asian immigrants, the rejection rate approached 18 percent. Medical exams were more comprehensive for those perceived as racially distinct.[20]

As early as the 1880s, philanthropic workers and immigrants themselves understood that child mortality and disease were related to housing conditions, economic status, and education. It was less clear how to remedy the situation. Reformers tried many tactics. In 1895 the Keep Clean Mission bathhouse opened in Milwaukee, using excess water from the beer-bottle sterilization process in the Schlitz Brewery next door to provide clean baths for children. Near Boston, the School of Outdoor Life offered a retreat for tubercular children. Of the first group of children admitted in 1909, two were American, twelve Irish, eleven Jewish, four Turkish, six Polish, and one Scottish. Conforming to the best medical practices of the time, the children ate healthy, substantial meals every day and took on housekeeping activities, especially gardening, that would keep them in the fresh air. They also bathed daily.[21] Children did tend to recover from tuberculosis more quickly in this protected environment, but they often relapsed upon returning home. Reformers understood that they would have to educate immigrants about disease and contagion if there were any hope of improving immigrant children's health.

Public health campaigns in the early twentieth century targeted immigrants by publishing pamphlets in English, German, Italian, and Yiddish on such topics as breast-feeding and pasteurizing milk. Many working-class mothers were in fact already breast-feeding their babies because it was both traditional and cheaper to do so. Few immigrant families had the iceboxes or refrigerators necessary for bottle feeding. For children drinking milk past infancy, the situation was more complicated.

American home economists found it disturbing that some immigrant children had so little access to milk. Studies found that Japanese children drank less than half the amount of milk that native-born American children drank daily. Reformers paid little attention to the fact that Japan was a non-milk-drinking society and instead concluded that all immigrant children suffered equally without ample milk provisions. To combat this problem, charitable organizations set up clean milk depots in every sizable city but often could not meet the demand. Immigrant children growing up on farms were much more likely to drink milk, though drinking unpasteurized milk carried its own risks, particularly in the summer.

Around the turn of the century, public health officials began to identify groups that seemed to have lower mortality rates so that they could encourage other immigrants to emulate them. These well-intentioned plans did not always work, however. For instance, the Jewish mortality rate was observably lower not only in the United States but also in Europe and Asia. Contemporary explanations always noted that Jewish mothers were less likely to work outside the home and more likely to breast-feed their children, which was considered a deterrent to disease. It also seemed possible that observing kosher dietary laws protected Jewish children from contaminated milk supplies, since they drank less milk. Even if these differences were factors, they were difficult to replicate. Most immigrant mothers could not afford not to work, which prevented them from prolonged breast-feeding. Non-Jewish families certainly were not about to keep kosher.

To the best of their abilities, parents tried to ward off disease and death. German and Russian immigrants continued their traditional practices of not giving babies solid food until they were a year old. This may have saved some lives, especially since food was so often spoiled by heat and flies. Immigrant parents also relied on folk healing practices to help their sick children. Ernesto Galarza recalled the *curandera* (healer) who came to his neighbor's home after the doctor had given up on a sick Mexican child. The *curandera* combined herbal medicine and prayers to the Virgin of Guadalupe.

> The little girl was uncovered. She lay naked, pale, and thin on the sheet, her arms straight down her sides. Around her the healer arranged a border of cactus leaves, which she took out of her satchel one by one, cutting them open around the edge. She warmed the cup with the powdered herbs and rubbed the concoction on the soles of the child's bare feet. With the paste, which she also warmed over the candle, the healer made a cross on the forehead of the patient and another on her chest.[22]

Even when they did not have such elaborate rituals as the Mexican *curandera*, many immigrants similarly drew on their own heritage of folk practices to fight the too common enemy of childhood disease. American doctors, even if they were willing to visit the tenements, seemed helpless in the face of such pervasive illness. Visiting nurses worked hard to change families' hygiene practices, but they often admitted defeat in the face of the appalling living conditions produced by poverty and overcrowding. Despite all their best efforts, for example, Italian boys and girls in New York remained far below the average height of American children, a statistic that public health officials saw as representative of poor nutrition and health care in the immigrant community.

A number of factors gradually led to a drop in infant mortality by the early twentieth century, though immigrants and other working-class families were the last to see the improvement. Declining fertility rates, even among Catholic immigrant families, helped parents allocate more resources to fewer children despite the obstacles they faced. Public health campaigns, from pure milk initiatives to hygiene education, ultimately had a salutary effect on standards of nutrition and health care. Advances in the urban infrastructure improved the physical environment of childhood by providing reliable sanitation, sewage, and water systems and even by demanding housing reforms.

Still, observers found plenty to deplore when confronted with immigrants' living conditions. Doctors, visiting nurses, teachers, social workers, and other representatives of American society and culture who came into frequent contact with immigrants expressed bewilderment and frustration at the starkly different perspectives on children they discovered. Many Italians, for instance, viewed wine as a natural food and appalled public health officials by freely giving it to their children to drink from about the age of two. Immigrant mothers were accused of endangering babies' health through ignorance and superstition. No amount of persuasion or explanation could convince one immigrant mother to let her two children be tested for tuberculosis, even though her husband and oldest child had died of the disease; she feared the procedure would make holes in their arms. As the director of New York's pure milk stations observed in frustration:

> The Italian mother who ties a string of coral beads around her badly-fed baby's wrist to make him get red blood . . . the Polish mother who packs her baby's soiled clothes in the bottom of a tub, sets him on them, and sozzles him with this water, from the bath . . . the Jewish mother who tries the formula that saved Mrs. Bobscheffsky's child on her own child—to its extinction—all require infinite patience and re-instruction.[23]

Within immigrant communities, forces for Americanization observed the differences between ethnic and American customs relating to children and encouraged immigrant parents to adopt American practices. "Do not give [children] intoxicating liquor," admonished the Slovakian A. G. Toth in his missive "How We Should Live in America," continuing, "Unfortunately I once saw a two-year-old boy drinking whiskey which his mother had given him and becoming an alcoholic like his father."[24] What was accept-

This woman probably had to fill the basin from a water pump outside her tenement, circa 1905. Since there were no closets in these buildings, clothes were often hung from nails. *(Library of Congress)*

able behavior barely worthy of comment in the Old World would not do in the New World. Immigrant girls learned in home economics classes how to sew more appropriate clothes for their baby siblings, who should no longer be tightly swaddled as in traditional practice. American child-rearing practices could theoretically not only prevent disease and death, a goal shared by all concerned, but also produce genuinely American children, a much more contested outcome.

The dire poverty and terrible living conditions of most urban immigrants led many of them to a natural interest in limiting the number of children they had, regardless of religious injunctions against birth control. Margaret Sanger's crusade for birth control began after she witnessed, while working as a visiting nurse in New York, the death of Sadie, a Jewish woman who had tried to perform an abortion on herself rather than bring another child into her desperately poor home. Sanger had already nursed this woman back to health after her successful attempt to abort an earlier pregnancy. She was so horrified when the doctor refused to offer Sadie any birth-control advice other than forcing her husband to sleep on the roof that she determined then and there to obtain the knowledge she did not yet have herself and disseminate it to those who needed the information most.

Without any knowledge of birth-control methods beyond folklore, immigrant parents had few choices other than abstinence to limit the size of their families. Life was so difficult in urban areas, and children were such economic burdens for even the very short period when they did not work, that babies were not always greeted with joy. Each child presented another set of challenges: Where would the baby sleep? What would the baby eat? What would the baby wear? Who could take care of the baby while other family members worked? The entrance of another child into a family could push a household past the razor-thin margin of poverty to starvation. Jacob Riis found that he could not judge the bitter man who consoled his wife about their dying infant with the words, "Hush, Mary! If we cannot keep the baby, need we complain—such as we?"[25]

Even in neighborhoods populated by immigrants who had achieved some measure of economic security, a too-large family represented a threat that had to be countered by whatever means possible. Kate Simon, growing up in the heavily Jewish, Italian, and Greek Bronx during the 1910s, where most of the children went to school and few of her classmates had more than two siblings, learned later that the widely accepted method of family size limitation used by the mothers in her neighborhood was abortion. The neighborhood children caught frequent glimpses of a Dr. James, who always seemed to visit their mothers when they were resting in bed. But they had no idea that he was on a mission to prevent septicemia or infanticide by providing safe abortions for minimal fees. Kate's own mother, grateful for "the work of the blessed hands of that wonderful old *goy*," had thirteen abortions—which she claimed was not the neighborhood record—rather than jeopardize her family's relatively comfortable life.[26]

Margaret Sanger and other birth-control activists found this situation intolerable. They were especially incensed that middle-class women surreptitiously circulated birth-control literature from Europe and had much greater access to information through their doctors than working-class women did. Although the Comstock laws against obscenity made disseminating birth-control information a crime, in 1916 Sanger nevertheless opened the first birth-control clinic in Brownsville, a Brooklyn suburb with a large population of Jews and Italians. She and her associates advertised the clinic in a series of pamphlets and handbills printed in Yiddish, Italian, and English. They were deluged by immigrant mothers hoping to improve the quality of life for their children by limiting their family size. The clinic was open only a few days before being closed down by state authorities, but the birth-control movement was under way.

Not everyone involved in spreading birth-control information to immigrant mothers acted out of purely charitable impulse. Sanger, among others, was also devoted to the so-called science of eugenics, which argued for racial caste systems and encouraged middle-class white women to have more children and working-class, immigrant, and African-American women to have fewer children. From Teddy Roosevelt to the deans of the new schools of social work appearing at institutions such as the University of Maryland and the University of Michigan, concerns over "race suicide" became very popular in response to the mass migrations into the United States at the turn of the century. Undoubtedly there was a sinister aspect to a movement that tried to dictate who should have children and how many they should have. Still, the desire of immigrants from a wide range of national and ethnic backgrounds to maximize their success in America by limiting family size made them natural, if uneasy, allies of the birth-control movement. From the immigrants' perspective, birth control led to better lives for the children they did have.

Resources in the Wider Community

Once immigrant children were born, their families could turn to communal resources for help, though often at a price. Especially in urban areas, a variety of agencies and programs developed to offer aid to poor infants and toddlers. Some institutions provided homes for abandoned children and orphans. Others offered child care so that mothers could go to work without resorting to such practices as tying small children to bedposts or table legs to keep them out of harm's way when they were left alone. As the personal, often religious nature of nineteenth-century philanthropy gradually evolved into the organizational, scientific approach to social work, the programs available to urban immigrants improved, but at the cost of the individualized relationships that volunteer charity workers had sometimes developed with their beneficiaries. On the other hand, some immigrant parents preferred to deal with a relatively faceless bureaucracy rather than admit their need and ask for help from a specific patron. Ethnic groups also created their own institutions to provide aid to children.

In all cases the overriding goal of the help offered to young immigrant children was Americanization. Nineteenth-century philanthropists and twentieth-century social workers shared the conviction that the best thing they could do for young immigrant children was to teach them how to act, speak, think, and live as Americans, by which they meant middle-class Americans. They fixed on young children's training as an effective way to reach not only the next generation but also the parents of the current one. As they saw it, the wider community had an interest in making sure that all these young newcomers to the American scene learned the correct lessons in the correct way in the correct time and at the correct place. Surely social peace and integration would follow.

Organizations and Institutions. Despite their ambivalent attitudes toward immigrant children, native-born Americans provided help of all kinds. Urban areas saw the most institutional help for children, as the greater concentration of immigrants there offered obvious centers of reform activity. Jane Addams's work with immigrants at Hull-House in Chicago was the most famous example of an urban settlement house, but similar institutions could be found in cities of any size. Cleveland's Alta House, funded by the Rockefellers, was typical in offering local Italian women both prenatal and baby clinics to improve the health of immigrant mothers and children. The Educational Alliance in New York, founded by members of the more established Jewish community, put together a program of classes, recreational activities, and opportunities for socialization. Jewish mothers could bring their babies to the Educational Alliance for limited medical care and also for infant classes that would teach them the most scientifically up-to-date ways to take care of their children.

Settlement houses and community centers like the Educational Alliance served one kind of immigrant population, and foundling homes and orphanages another. Institutional care took a variety of forms and changed dramatically during the period from 1880 to 1925. In some states the legal system supported immigrant children by trying to respect their families' religious preferences. As early as 1875, New York's Children's Law provided that children should be committed to institutional care run by representatives of the same religious faith as their parents. The law was dropped in 1876 but reinstated in 1878 and then emulated by other states. From 1899 on, Illinois state law also required the courts to place children in the care of individuals or institutions with the same religious beliefs as the parents.

At the Foundling Asylum of Sisters of Charity in New York, mothers could leave the infants they were unable to care for. The Sisters of Charity asked no questions and required only that mothers dropping off babies stay long enough to nurse their own child and another infant before leaving. At four or five years of age, the children left by their mothers were usually sent west for adoption through Charles Loring Brace's Children's Aid Society. The large orphanages and institutions so demonized by Charles Dickens and others in the mid- to late nineteenth century persisted, but alternatives developed. Young children whose families could not or would not support them were increasingly placed in private homes rather than institutions. In 1910, New York's Hebrew Orphan Asylum and Hebrew Sheltering Guardian Society maintained institutional homes but also placed out nearly five hundred Jewish children in private homes. Boarding families responded to advertisements in Jewish newspapers or were recommended by charitable organizations and personal references. A full-time agent evaluated all the applicants and rejected most of them, trying to ensure that the children would not be put to hard labor or otherwise abused. New York's Board of Health also supervised the placements and insisted that the families have sources of income other than the payments they received for taking in dependent children. All the children attended public schools and, in keeping with the religious nature of their original placement, typically attended Jewish educational classes as well.

The practice of boarding out children became fairly popular on the East Coast but was less common in the Midwest. Critics

Sister Irene and her flock in the New York Foundling Asylum, 1888, photograph by Jacob Riis. *(Library of Congress)*

charged that the supervision of placements was inadequate and that dependent children, especially infants and toddlers who could not speak for themselves, suffered at the hands of mercenary mothers who saw them as sources of income rather than individuals in need of care. Charitable and social service organizations also found it easier to raise money for visible institutional buildings than a network of boarding placements. Still, many agreed that young children would certainly thrive better in a home atmosphere than an institutional one, and over several decades boarding out remained a viable option.

Immigrant communities accustomed to death, desertion, and disease devised their own strategies for caring for young children. Churches sponsored preschools so that mothers would not have to take their children to work or leave them home alone. These preschools proved highly popular, with Greenwich Village's parish of Pompei serving ninety toddlers a day as soon as it opened early in the twentieth century, for example. The Catholic church provided in many ways for immigrant children. In 1901 the Detroit-based Order of Felician Sisters alone ran thirty-nine Polish parochial institutions all over the United States, including the St. Clara Institution for Orphan Boys in Polonia, Wisconsin, the St. Felix boardinghouse for orphan girls in Detroit, the Immaculate Heart of Mary orphanage in Buffalo, and the St. Joseph Immigrant House in New York.

Nonreligious organizations also sponsored institutions for young immigrants. The Japanese Humane Society of Los Angeles established the Shonien, an orphanage for dependent Japanese children that received state licensure in 1916, two years after its founding. In emergencies the Shonien admitted Chinese and Mexican children as well. As one nurse explained, the Shonien took the place of the grandmothers who in Japan would take care of young children. In "California, no grandmothers. Japan, grandmothers care for babies. California, mamas all brides, grandma in Japan." The immigration restrictions that had kept Japanese women out of the United States for so long resulted in very few extended families. In 1900 there were only 410 married Japanese women out of a population of 24,326 first-generation Issei and second-generation Nisei in America.[27] The community had to provide the care that extended families had customarily provided. All these ethnic institutions served as stark reminders of what immigrants had left behind and what they were able to build within a generation in their new home.

The Kindergarten Movement. Not even the youngest children living, playing, or learning in institutions set up by outsiders or insiders were too young to face what might be called a preschool identity conflict. Rose Carini, who at the age of five left Italy with her mother to join her father in Milwaukee, was at first terrified of kindergarten. She remembered, "They registered me and I cried. I did not want to leave my mother because first of all I didn't speak English. My parents didn't either."[28] Bill Hosokawa attended a public school in Seattle where 98 percent of the students were the American-born children of Japanese parents. Yet when he began kindergarten around 1920, he recalled,

> On the day I was dragged, reluctant and apprehensive, to a kindergarten class at the Old Main Street School in Seattle, the only language I understood was Japanese. English was so foreign to my ears that I hardly knew my newly acquired first name. Until a few days earlier it had been Kumpei, an uncommon Japanese name . . . but after consulting friends, my father added the solidly Anglo-Saxon William to help my teacher cope with the problem of introducing me to the American educational system.[29]

In this case, Kumpei/William's parents and, apparently, all his neighbors were clearly interested in using the public schools to integrate their Japanese-American children into public American life. That choice, however, left small children bewildered and confused about everything from language to their own names.

As far as many advocates of kindergarten were concerned, this confusion, which they assumed would resolve itself in favor of the dominant American culture, was beneficial. Richard Gilder, president of the New York Kindergarten Association, wrote in 1903, "The kindergarten age marks our earliest opportunity to catch the little Russian, the little Italian, the little German, Pole, Syrian and the rest and begin to make good American citizens of them." Gilder expressed supreme confidence that early childhood education would not only transform immigrant children into Americans but also improve the tenor of their family life. He and other kindergarten advocates suggested such practices as playing games with the children to teach them how to wash their hands and brush their teeth. "The whole family," Gilder wrote, "comes under the influence of what I may call the kindergarten charm" as the young

The American flag in the background symbolizes the acculturation demanded of immigrant children from the very moment of their arrival on
Ellis Island—here upon their first Christmas in America, 1918. *(Library
of Congress)*

children introduced the manners and morals they learned at school
into their family homes.[30]

The Bureau of Education of the U.S. Department of the Inte-
rior agreed with such sentiments, advising kindergarten teachers to
direct their efforts at both their young charges and their mothers by
paying home visits and conducting mothers' meetings. Educators
recognized that immigrant mothers were often the last members of
families to acquire the language skills and cultural knowledge critical to socialization. They hoped to use mothers' close connections
to their young children to develop the "friendly give-and-take rela-

tions which ought to exist between the older Americans and the foreign neighbor."[31] Immigrants and educators alike could see the consequences of educating small children. Immigrant families had to decide whether to send their children outside their families and communities for education—and, if so, whether to join them there as proposed by the kindergarten movement—or to keep their children close by, both figuratively and literally. It was difficult to strike a balance, but infancy and early childhood were only the first in a series of battlegrounds over identity, affiliation, and acculturation.

CHAPTER THREE

At School, at Work, at Home, at Play

Miss Hopley and her teachers never let us forget why we were at Lincoln [School]: for those who were alien, to become good Americans; for those who were so born, to accept the rest of us. Off the school grounds, we traded the same insults we heard from our elders. On the playground we were sure to be marched up to the principal's office for calling someone a wop, a chink, a dago, or a greaser. The school was not so much a melting pot as a griddle where Miss Hopley and her helpers warmed knowledge into us and roasted racial hatreds out of us.

—Ernesto Galarza, "Barrio Boy" (1971)[1]

❧ BY THE TIME Ernesto Galarza entered Lincoln School's doors, he had already been through a good deal for a child. He and his mother had left Mexico in 1910 to escape the onset of the Mexican Revolution and ended up settling in Sacramento, where two of her brothers already lived. The Galarza family traveled to the United States by stagecoach, a very different sort of migration journey than those of the European and Asian immigrants who crossed the oceans. They rented a furnished apartment and gradually began to venture out into their new neighborhood. He and his mother took walks around the state capitol, which they admiringly referred to as "El Capitolio." Ernesto liked the fact that so much of the commercial activity and social bustle of the *barrio* was conducted in Spanish. Within the radius of a few blocks were Mexican grocery stores, saloons, and other businesses catering to the Mexican immigrant community. Yet within those same few blocks were a Chinese restaurant, a Japanese movie theater, a Filipino billiards parlor, and a Hindu boardinghouse. Many nationalities met and mingled in the *barrio* where young Ernesto lived. They developed separate networks for job referrals, apartment rentals, and charitable associations, but they also all bought the same boxes of corn flakes and bottles of Karo syrup, identifying the products by the pictures on the packaging and quickly becoming used to new foods like oatmeal.

Ernesto's mother and uncles retained a number of Mexican traditions at home. They ate rice and beans, spoke Spanish, and participated in the annual *Cinco de Mayo* celebrations. They relied on other Mexican immigrants with a better command of English to help them when they needed to see a doctor or go to court or fill out a money order. By the time Ernesto finished third grade, he was earning a regular wage by performing these services for neighbors willing to pay for his help. He learned English at school, which his mother insisted he attend even though she knew that her son might be taught to reject the ethnic customs she found so comforting. But she saw the difficulty her Spanish-speaking brothers had in finding and keeping jobs, and she wanted a brighter future for her son.

At first Ernesto was quite nervous about going to school. He felt better when he met his classmates, who came from Irish, Japanese, Korean, Portuguese, Italian, Yugoslavian, American, and Polish families. The first-grade teacher gave special instruction to the non-English speakers, vowing to teach them so thoroughly that no one would ever guess their immigrant origins by listening to them speak. The school principal introduced her students to Sacramento personages like a police sergeant and the fire chief so that the children would feel connected to the city where they lived. Regardless of background, all the students saluted the American flag and sang "My County 'Tis of Thee" every morning. They were addressed by their ethnic names, but in school, at least, no other vestige of foreign allegiance was tolerated.

Like hundreds of thousands of other immigrant children, Ernesto navigated the sometimes perilous waters of multiple cultures and multiple identities. Sometimes his Mexican origins seemed most important, as when he attended the frequent fiestas punctuating the social calendar of the Sacramento *barrio*. Sometimes his American environs appeared most central to his experience, as when he insisted his mother buy him proper American clothing so he would not be embarrassed at school. The fact that he was a boy allowed him significantly greater freedom to wander the neighborhood than a girl would have had. The fact that his mother was the head of the household in his father's absence threw more economic responsibility on his young shoulders, and by the age of eight he began to work after school and during the summers. As expected of him, Ernesto attended church services and was regarded as an altar boy candidate by his Spanish-speaking priest. At the same time he considered joining the Sacramento Boys' Band with his mixed group of schoolmates. Without thinking about it very deeply at the time, Ernesto spent his childhood bridging cultures, a very common experience for immigrant children.

Although many aspects of American life changed during the period of mass immigration, it was also true that most of the structures and conflicts that shaped immigrant children's lives remained in place. All immigrant families brought specific ethnic and cultural values with them, and few were willing to abandon them wholesale. This presented children with problems if their families' traditions clashed with the American values pressed upon them by well-meaning but insistent teachers or employers. Their very success in adapting to the new American life their families had chosen might also make them a disappointment in traditional terms. These kinds of conflicts became particularly apparent in school settings, where immigrant children learned quickly that even conforming in every way would not save them from stereotyping and discrimination. While it could be reassuring, as Ernesto felt, to go to school with children facing similar challenges, prejudice existed just as much among various ethnic groups as between native-born Americans and immigrants. The presence of these problems in schools transformed the nature of public education in the early twentieth century.

Immigrant parents fought back against the Americanizing effects of public schools. Although they wanted their children to succeed—indeed, that was a primary motivation for their decision to emigrate—they felt strongly about preserving their traditional culture. They deployed all kinds of strategies to maintain tradition, including establishing language schools and celebrating holidays in ways that endeared cultural traditions to their children's hearts. Immigrant children responded positively to the holiday celebrations, if less so to the language schools, but in the increasingly diverse social environment of urban America, in particular, a great deal of cultural mixing across background was inevitable. Whether at work, on the streets, or at school, immigrant children shared experiences with one another that differed from both the experiences of their families and their native-born peers.

Shop Floors and School Yards

Because relatively few immigrants arrived in the United States with sufficient resources to provide immediately comfortable, secure lives for their children, it is hardly surprising that finding and keeping jobs became a priority for immigrants of all ages. Few families could manage on the salary of just one person, and native-born children were already commonly members of the American workforce. Progressive reformers attacked child labor as dangerous and immoral, but most immigrants could not afford to support or obey child-labor laws that limited their families' earning potential and were not upheld by the state in most cases anyway. Even if they also attended school, most working-class children in America at the turn of the century contributed in some way to the family economy.

Despite the expectation that their children would add economic value to the household, immigrant parents also tried to provide some kind of education, though definitions of what comprised a solid education differed greatly among ethnic groups. For some immigrants, free public education was a major attraction of the United States. Professional educators, reformers, and social observers believed that schools were responsible for turning out the best possible American citizens and as such were obliged to Americanize the hordes of immigrant children passing through their halls. Immigrant parents viewed schools with wary eyes, torn between providing education for their children as native-born parents did and fearing the family consequences of such blatant Americanization. Children themselves expressed some ambivalence about schools. On one hand, many saw education as their path toward greater knowledge, economic success, and cultural integration than their parents could ever achieve. On the other hand, many experienced severe discrimination at school or failed to see the value of "book learning" for the kinds of lives they were likely to have as adults. Like work, education became a fundamental but ambivalent part of immigrant children's lives.

Child Labor. Virtually all immigrant families operated as economic units. Although not every immigrant family arrived impoverished—the most impoverished would not have been able to afford migration—few had sufficient resources to enjoy a financial cushion. Work became an immediate part of daily life. Immigrants often

These immigrant boys attended night school in Boston, 1909, after working all day. *(Library of Congress)*

looked for work within days of arrival, usually relying on personal connections to help them find their first jobs. With the exception of highly skilled craftsmen, immigrants typically performed the least skilled work for the lowest pay within a given labor market. Only in the rare case could one person's wages support a family. An 1881 study conducted by the Pennsylvania Department of Internal Affairs found that of 142 workers and their families, not one father's earnings equaled the entire earnings of the rest of the family for the year. For example, one miner with five children earned $80 in 1881, but his total family income was more than $800 because of the children's labor.[2] A Slavic family's budget in pre–World War I Pennsylvania assumed that, even with several family members working, their wages would come to less than $12 a week. The family budgeted $4.64 for food, $1.62 for rent, $1.57 for clothing, and less than $1 a week each for fuel, housekeeping, tobacco, liquor, furniture, and insurance. There was no provision at all in this tight budget for medicine.[3]

Only the collective wages of several family members could ensure survival. Poverty was pervasive among immigrant families. In Gary, Indiana, Italian laborer Mike Taje described his family's dire straits in stark terms: "Got-a seven kid. Angelo have no got shoe, Rose no got-a shirt. Michelo got-a da breeches, Pete no got-a shirt. Can no buy. I'm work dollar feefty cent day."[4] Given these circumstances, it is not surprising that in 1870 the government estimated that one of eight children between ten and fifteen was gainfully employed. This proportion rose by 1900 to one of six. Although these numbers assumed that 60 percent of these children worked in agricultural jobs, that was probably a major underestimate, since the counts did not include children who worked on family farms.[5] At the turn of the century, children participated in the transformation of family farms to large commercial agricultural interests by providing an important part of the workforce making the transition from chores to wage labor.

Women's domestic roles affected work patterns, with urban immigrant women more likely to serve as household managers, take in boarders, and perform homework such as tatting lace, making matchboxes, or cracking nuts than seek employment outside the home. That left children to fill in the economic gap left by their fathers' inadequate wages or, in some cases, absence from the household. Russian immigrant Maurice Hindus's childhood experience was common.

> Only by pooling our earnings together, and with [Mother] in charge of the housekeeping, could we have the meat and the butter and the other foods that we ate, and of which I had eloquently boasted in letters to former schoolmates in Russia.[6]

As was the case for Maurice and his siblings, family cooperation in economic matters meant that immigrant children were likely to work from a young age.

Immigrant families were not alone in requiring multiple wages for household support, of course. Poor families of all racial and ethnic backgrounds operated in much the same way, though a variety of factors came into play. In the South, African-American children were even more likely to work than immigrant children. In Northern cities like Philadelphia and Providence, however, African-American children were less likely to work than immigrant children, and fewer jobs were open to them. Instead African-American women worked and the children attended school. Urban black communities took married women's work for granted and prioritized children's schooling, since they had more educational opportunity in the North than in the South.

All working children could contribute in a number of ways. They took jobs either after or instead of school. They helped their mothers with homework like making artificial flowers or rolling cigars. They gave up living space for boarders. They brought scrap coal and wood into their homes as fuel. Boys performed tasks in mines or fields that required small bodies. Girls left home for jobs as domestic servants and turned their wages over to the family. In all these ways, immigrant children played critical roles in household finances.

Working children's most immediate sacrifice was formal education. The Polish children who worked 60 hours a week in Pennsylvania coal mines clearly had neither time nor opportunity to attend school while earning their $2.68 weekly wage.[7] In one coal-mining town, no boy over age thirteen was in school because at eleven or twelve years, Polish boys began going to the mines with their fathers or other male relatives. Ten percent of the workforce consisted of underage boys.[8] By one count, 12.7 percent of first-generation Italian children in New York between the ages of six and fifteen were at

A Polish boy picks berries on a farm near Baltimore, 1909. The stooped position required in agricultural work could lead to serious health problems. *(Library of Congress)*

work rather than in school.[9] In 1911 in eastern Pennsylvania, children earned 65 percent of the family incomes among unskilled Irish immigrants and 46 percent of the family incomes among unskilled Polish immigrants. Even among skilled immigrants, the comparable numbers were 35 percent for the Irish and 40 percent for the Polish.[10] Mexican families working the southern California citrus harvest earned only $600 to $800 a year, even with their children's wages.[11] These families would not have survived without their children's earnings. Children understood this reality, but that did not necessarily ease their pain at being denied an education. Rose

A boy unable to speak a word of English worked at this factory in Chicopee, Massachusetts, in 1911. *(Library of Congress)*

Cohen, who went to work in New York's garment industry immediately after arriving in the United States, could not hide her envy of her more fortunate contemporaries. "In their white summery dresses and with books under their arm," she recalled, "they appeared to me like wonderful little beings of a world entirely different from mine."[12]

Some child labor occurred within a slightly separate labor market. Immigrant children did the jobs too brief or too menial for adults, such as rolling milk cans, mixing syrups, collecting rags, and running errands. Young boys worked as lookouts so back-alley gambling could carry on without interruption. Children doing this kind of work might be paid in food or other goods rather than money, so these jobs were likely to be after-school occupations rather than full-time work. But other children worked in regular employment settings. Pauline Newman recalled of her job in the New York garment industry:

> It was a child's work, since we all were children. We had a corner in the factory which was like a kindergarten. The work wasn't difficult. The shirtwaist finished by the [sewing machine] operator could come to us, so we could cut off the thread left by the needle of the machine. You had a little scissor because you were children.[13]

The daughter of an Italian baker also worked in an adult work environment: her home, where her mother made jeweler's chains.

> We were raised to work every minute. When a child was 5 or 6 and could hold a plier, my mother would sit us around the table and we would link jewelry. We'd link chains and rosary beads or mesh purses. It was like a game. Visiting kids would sit down and link in our house. Whoever did the most would get some extra snack or candy or fruit.

Her mother made two to four dollars a week with the help of her children and their friends.[14] Family businesses also relied on children's work. Ralph and Charles Borrelli sold soft drinks at the Italian theater their father opened in Philadelphia after emigrating from Naples. They also played any children's parts in the theater's productions. Although their father rarely paid them cash, the Borrelli brothers' work nonetheless contributed to family finances by saving their father from paying others wages for the same work.

One of the more visible jobs held by children, almost exclusively boys, was that of the newsboy. Some boys served regular paper routes, but these were typically native-born boys who delivered newspapers as an after-school job. Immigrant boys were much more likely to work full time as newsboys, standing on street corners until they had sold every one of their papers, often late into the night. Newsboys were so pervasive on urban streets that in many cities they eventually organized themselves, in a few cases even conducting successful strikes against the middlemen newspaper suppliers who looked for any excuse to cheat their young contract workers. As in other cities, in Milwaukee the boys formed the Newsboys' Republic with the blessing of the city fathers. All members of the Republic were supposed to have permits from the Milwaukee Street Trades Commission. They divided the city into districts along ethnic lines, since "Tony of the Italian district, and Isidore of the Russian Jews, are far better able to look after their fellow 'newsies' than the adult policemen of Irish birth." Selling corners were protected, and self-regulation kept boys out of the juvenile court system. Urban reformers in Milwaukee applauded this show of initiative by the newsboys and considered it a sign of acculturation, even among a population with relatively limited exposure to more formal Americanization efforts. As the reform-minded national periodical *The Outlook* noted approvingly in 1913, "When one considers the cosmopolitan character of Milwaukee's population, this little democracy, with its American Chief Justice, its German President, and its Russian Jew Vice-President, becomes an important agent for the assimilation of our second and third generations of foreigners."[15]

Rural immigrant children worked too. Only the rare Norwegian girl escaped employment as either a *barnepiges* (nursemaid) or *tjenestepiges* (maid-of-all-work) at some point in her young life. Japanese children in California worked in farm fields or in city gardens. They also manned roadside stands where they sold the literal fruits of their families' labor. In Colorado and Nebraska, farmers hired entire families of Germans from Russia to harvest their beets. Beet harvesting was a three-step process involving thinning, hoeing, and topping. Children worked on their hands and knees to thin the beets to six inches between the plants; their mothers sewed padding into their trousers to try to protect their knees. These families earned ten to fifteen dollars an acre for the summer's work.

Whether they worked in fields or factories, in cities or on farms, with family members or alone, immigrant children were affected by the waves of unrest sweeping working-class America during the late nineteenth and early twentieth centuries. Once they began to work, immigrant children found themselves being politicized on the job. When Pauline Newman began working for her union at the age of fifteen, she was so young that she received front-page publicity for her activities. She did not consider herself too young, however, since she had already been working for years.

Once the 1912 textile workers' strike began in Lawrence, Massachusetts, dozens of children without enough to eat were sent from there to sympathetic Italian families in New York during what became known as the "Exodus of the Children." Those who stayed home, like ten-year-old Philip Bonacorsi, read newspaper accounts of the strike to their parents. Living in a town like Lawrence also politicized children. During the 1919 walkout there, children stayed home from school to help their striking parents and siblings in a show of family solidarity. Theresa Campagne got in trouble at school for wearing a dress with Industrial Workers of the World (IWW) buttons that her sister made for her.

If household economics did not allow for children's full-time education, the families attempted to arrange combinations of work and education. Social investigators in Chicago reported that two Finnish children, a ten-year-old boy and a seven-year-old girl, attended school every day but spent their afternoons and evenings tending bar at their father's saloon so he would have to pay only part-time wages to a nonfamily member. This combination led to long and weary days. In 1922 the U.S. Children's Bureau reported that children who worked after school were typically tired, listless, and poorly developed.

Rural families developed their own strategies for combining work and education. The children of German-Russian beet farmers in Colorado did not go to school until after the harvest was over be-

During a 1912 strike in Lawrence, Massachusetts, children carry luggage and wear tags as they prepare to leave the city during the "Exodus of the Children." *(Library of Congress)*

cause they were needed in the fields. A few went to summer school every day after thinning and topping the beets, but teachers complained that their students could neither learn nor stay awake after long hours of physical labor. Beginning around 1910, some Colorado school districts took steps to keep children in school and avoid sudden overcrowding when the farmers' children showed up at the schoolhouses after the harvest. They started school in early August, closed during the harvest season starting in October, then reopened after the beet season had ended for the year.

Children were willing to find gainful employment if that would allow them to expand their educational activity, no matter how hard it was to combine work and schooling. The first thing the Paik family did upon arriving in their mining town was to locate the schoolhouse, a one-room building with a single teacher for all eight grades. Mary and her brother Meung were the only Korean students among a group of Mexican students. But as soon as she went to school, Mary went to work. The supervisor of the mining camp that supported the school paid her twenty-five cents a day to clean the schoolhouse and the outhouse, chop firewood for the school stove, and ring the bell every morning. She also worked in the local boardinghouse kitchen every night, earning another twenty-five cents daily to help prepare meals for the unmarried men living in the mining town. The Paik family depended on both Mary's wages and the leftover meat and bread she brought home. She managed to transform her combination of work and education into something that would benefit both her family and herself.

The vexed relationship between work and schooling was one of many factors that led late-nineteenth- and early-twentieth-century educators to conclude that the best form of schooling was vocational education. If working-class children had to work sooner rather than later, they should have educational experiences that prepared them for more important, more lucrative work. Although supported by many progressive educators, vocational education also lined up neatly with some immigrant parents' utilitarian attitude toward education as valuable only as a means toward achieving economic success.

While social utility seemed a noble educational goal, in practice supporters of vocational education held mixed motives. The Philadelphia school board pushed vocational education on immigrant children and African-American children "to prevent children from becoming misfits in the world of industry," a concern the school board apparently did not apply to native-born white children.[16] Planters in Hawaii feared that too much classical education would spoil their future supply of agricultural labor. When asked about the benefits of opening more schools for Japanese children, one planter on Maui said, "Oh, yes, they'll make intelligent citizens all right enough, but not plantation laborers—and that's what we want."[17] Planters were more likely to support vocational education as matching the goals they had for the Japanese and Korean children of their workforce.

Vocational education was a larger issue for adolescents than for elementary school children, but the need of many working-class families to combine their children's work and education meant that parents were also likely to support it, though not for the same reasons. The Japanese and Korean parents who worked for that Maui planter almost certainly wanted more for their children than another generation of agricultural labor. The only way they knew to achieve that goal was to provide their children with an education, even if combined with work in the context of the family economy. Some Italian parents, on the other hand, unhappy about the role of American schools in prolonging children's dependence, welcomed vocational training as a better match for their own educational priorities of practical skills and independence. Especially in relation to work, education carried multiple meanings.

Immigrant Children at School. The most common provider of education to immigrant children, no matter how defined, was the public school. Late-nineteenth- and early-twentieth-century mass immigration exerted an immediate impact on American public education. The number of immigrant children pouring into schools had profound consequences. The U.S. Immigration Commission's 1911 report on immigrant children in school studied 2,036,376 schoolchildren, 1,815,217 of them in public schools in 37 states, and 221,159 in parochial schools in 24 cities. This number was by no means a full count.[18] By 1908, 71.5 percent of the students in New York public schools were either foreign born or the children of immigrant parents.[19] A study estimated that in 1917, 30 percent of schoolchildren in New York were of Italian parentage.[20] Even in the mining town of Bingham Canyon, Utah, the school served a population of 200 students who among them spoke 27 languages.[21] When Pardee Lowe entered school in San Francisco, his teacher attached nationalities to the names when she took attendance, calling out, "Louisa Fleischner—Austrian" and "Yuri Matsuyama—Japanese." Of the 16 students in Pardee's class, no two were of the same nationality.

Diversity of background was not matched by diversity in other areas, however. The U.S. Immigration Commission found that more than half the foreign-born schoolchildren in the study were under six years of age when they came to the United States. Only 10 percent of them were over ten on arrival. These numbers demonstrated that children were far more likely to go to school if they were younger when they immigrated, illustrating an important disparity in access to education. The numbers held true even within families, meaning that younger children were always more likely to attend school, and to attend for longer periods of time, than their older siblings.[22] The schools themselves bore some responsibility for the uneven distribution of age. Even when they offered beginner classes, they often started them only in the fall, so children arriving throughout the rest of the year would have to wait to begin school. These children could easily lose momentum, and the older they were, the more likely they were to go to work instead. Joseph Baccardo, who left Italy when he was ten years old, tried to go to school after joining his father in Philadelphia. But his father needed him to work every spring and summer, so his attendance was sporadic at best. The other students also mocked his greenhorn clothing and manners, and he soon gave up the idea of going to school.

Social investigators proposed remedies for unequal access to education. The Chicago sociologists Edith Abbott and Sophonisba Breckinridge suggested that the names and ages of all immigrant children arriving in the United States be sent to school authorities

Gary, Indiana, schoolchildren were probably posed to demonstrate the diverse school population of a mill town that prided itself on its progressive school system. Front row, left to right: Scotch, Russian, Irish, Assyrian, Slavic, Jewish, Spanish. Middle row: American, Austrian, German, Bulgarian. Back row: Greek, Negro, Romanian, Lithuanian, Italian, Polish, Croatian, Hungarian. *(Miriam and Ira D. Wallach Division, New York Public Library, Astor, Lenox and Tilden Foundations)*

at their final destinations so that their parents could be immediately informed about compulsory education laws. This idea was never implemented, as both parents and school officials had an interest in less rigid educational systems. Parents might not be able to afford to send their children to school, and officials were already overwhelmed by the effects of mass immigration. Rapid population growth led to terrible overcrowding. In Buffalo in 1916, one school built for 1,020 students served 8,273. Thirty-nine percent of Buffalo classrooms had insufficient floor area, with 54 percent lacking adequate air space and 74 percent lacking adequate windows.[23]

The diversity in American classrooms at the turn of the century led to both the creation of ethnic stereotypes and the reinforcement of those already in circulation. In 1901 the U.S. Industrial Commission reported matter-of-factly that "the Italian children are more or less difficult to discipline and irresponsible. . . . They are fair students, better than the Irish, but not as good as the Hebrews and the Germans at book work."[24] Observing New York's P.S. 1 in 1903, the writer A. R. Dugmore commented:

Although the school is democratic, and although the public school has taught them the English language and a certain feeling of Americanism, their race shows itself often in the classroom. For example, the Russian and Polish Jews have a school standing far out of proportion to their number, and the Italians are unquestionably the most artistic in the manual training shops, while, as we have seen, the Irish talent for leadership and organization is not impaired by the public school.[25]

Such observations reflected both preconceptions about different groups and conclusions drawn from educators' actual experiences.

Studies of different groups that claimed scientific objectivity were even more problematic. A report on American-born Japanese children who had attended American schools for at least four years concluded that their average IQ was 90.2, compared with Northern Europeans' average of 100.3, Finns' of 90, Slovaks' of 85.6, and Italians' of 77.5.[26] The educational psychologist William A. Sheldon presented similar findings in 1924, with his intelligence tests showing the IQ of American children at 100, Hebrews at 98, Chinese at 90, Mexicans at 85, Italians at 77, and Negroes at 75.[27] Given the racial hierarchies accepted as scientific at the time, the data were hardly surprising. These figures did not go undisputed, though only rarely did dissenters level charges of racism against the social scientists. Instead they pointed to their own experience and argued that there was no intellectual difference among children of different backgrounds. Mr. Knox, principal of a school in San Antonio with a 90 percent Mexican population, also resisted the idea that intelligence or ability were linked to skin color. When interviewed, he insisted, "Many of my best students are of the darkest types."[28]

If not in agreement about differential abilities, where the Sheldons and Knoxes of the world could concur was on the relative attitudes of different groups toward education. In rural areas the tendency of most ethnic groups to live in insular, ethnically homogeneous communities allowed easy comparison of investment in educational resources. For example, in 1911 in South Dakota, predominantly Norwegian counties had only one school while German-Russians had twelve. German-Russian representatives were only too happy to boast of their superior commitment to education.[29] In urban areas, attitudes toward education were also measured by length of school attendance. By 1910 fewer than 10 percent of Italian, Polish, and Slovakian children stayed in school past sixth grade in Chicago and Cleveland.[30] Although obviously the need for children's wages contributed greatly to the very low number of these students who continued their formal education, social observers at the time wondered how poor Jewish and Swedish children could stay in school given their families' similarly dire financial straits. The answer, they concluded, was a different attitude toward the goals and purposes of education.

The two groups most often contrasted for their different attitudes toward education were the Jews and the Italians. The *Jewish Daily Forward* reported with pride that

to the list of Jewish holidays should be added another important holiday, graduation day. . . . In fact, to the proud Jew, reflecting somewhat partially on the splendid representation of Jewish children in the commencement rituals, it seems as if commencement day is an institution for the exhibition of Jewish love for knowledge.[31]

In cities across the United States, Jewish children did in fact stay in school longer than virtually any other ethnic group, though family economic need played a role for them too, and high school education was not as common as elementary school education. This school success was much commented upon by educators and the public, whose approval was based in part on the perceived willingness of Jewish parents to encourage Americanization though schooling. Equally commented upon, though with disapproval, was the apparent aversion of Italians to educating their children, and, by extension, countenancing Americanization. Even sympathetic observers like settlement house workers and social workers believed that Italian families felt threatened by public schools that emphasized citizenship and belonging to the larger society over family membership. The traditional Italian goal of raising children who were *ben educato* was rooted in values, attitudes, and skills related to family life and had little to do with formal education.

It is true that in much of Italian-American fiction, school appeared as a harmful or ineffectual institution. But it is also true that Italians were no more monolithic a group than any other in their attitudes toward education. *L'Italia*, an important Chicago Italian newspaper, supported compulsory education in Chicago and opposed rag picking and other children's economic activities in the street. Leonardo Covello's parents sent him to school days after arriving in the United States. More important than these examples, Italian parents' attitudes toward education may have been one practical response to the harsh economic realities of life in America. As their situation changed, so did their educational strategies, resulting in the long term (by the 1950s) in considerably more educational parity between Italians and Jews.

Making Good Americans. Although students and parents might have brought different attitudes toward education with them into the classroom, educators in the late nineteenth and early twentieth centuries were far more likely to share the belief that schools should function as agents of Americanization. As one author put it in 1920, "The moment the child crosses the threshold of the schoolhouse, the question of his future fealty is settled."[32] A report on a Thanksgiving celebration for young children in Milwaukee that same year observed with satisfaction, "Eager-faced little Hebrews, large-eyed and serene young Germans . . . learned this first lesson of Americanization well."[33] Indeed, many children learned that the only path to success was rapid acculturation, and when the rewards included new clothes, soda pop, ice cream, automobiles, and skyscrapers, as one Jewish girl in Milwaukee believed, resistance seemed not only futile but foolhardy.

Still, Americanization was a contested project on all sides. Children themselves were not sure what constituted acculturation or assimilation. As one Italian boy explained, "It never occurred to me that just being a citizen of the United States meant that I was an 'American.' 'Americans' were people who ate peanut butter and jelly on mushy white bread . . ."[34] Immigrant parents were often equally ambivalent. For example, the Blom children in Minnesota went to public school but learned Swedish at home from their parents, who also planned to send them to a Swedish-speaking Lutheran pastor for religious instruction. The insistence of most ethnic groups on maintaining some form of language school was only one example of widespread resistance to radical assimilation. At the same time few immigrant parents wished to deny the children the benefits of America—those very benefits were the reason why many of them had traveled to their new country. Recognition of the positive effects of Americanization spread even among those who might otherwise be seen as the most conservative elements of immigrant communities. For instance, many Mexican children in the Southwest were encouraged by their Catholic teachers, including nuns, to adapt themselves to American life.

The ambivalence was clear in an episode Jacob Riis recounted in his contribution to the 1895 anthology *The Poor in Great Cities*. Riis told the tale of an Upper East Side classroom in New York City that adopted the custom of saluting the American flag to inculcate patriotism in the immigrant student population. In order to train the children in democratic ways, the teachers first conducted a vote so the students could choose whether to salute the flag. Most of them voted to salute, but five Bohemian students did not. One of them, a little girl, brought the flag of her homeland and voted to salute that flag instead. Riis noted with approval that the teacher explained freedom of expression to the class, and from then on, every morning all the students except one saluted the American flag and then watched courteously as the girl paid homage to her Bohemian banner.[35] This episode was one of accommodation, acculturation, and resistance all at once, and demonstrated the complex nature of Americanization.

The process took countless forms. Not everyone would have agreed with the Los Angeles school superintendent's 1917 comment that educating immigrant children was primarily to ensure "that they might not be a menace to the city of Los Angeles," but most schools with immigrant populations incorporated the same penny lunch, after-hours playground, and home-visit program that the Los Angeles schools offered immigrant children.[36] In Placerville, Idaho, a teacher assigned native-born girls the task of shampooing their Chinese classmates, whose traditional hairstyles were hard to create and thus were washed less frequently than American standards of hygiene would dicate. Similarly, Molokan girls from the

Transcaucasus region of Russia traditionally wore shawls as a symbol of their purity, but Los Angeles city officials banned the shawls from school because they supposedly harbored disease and lice. Foreign hairstyles and shawls marked an obvious difference between immigrant and American girls that well-meaning proponents of Americanization were unwilling to let stand. Of course, not all immigrant children resented the discipline of Americanization. Pardee Lowe loved his teacher for playing games and telling stories but also for giving her students baths twice weekly. Since there were no bathing facilities at home, he and his family were more than happy to overlook any impugning of their sanitary standards and take advantage of the program.

Ernesto Galarza's elementary school experiences exemplified the promise of Americanization through education. As soon as his family settled in America in the early 1910s, his mother tried to make him feel better about the changes in his young life by explaining his new country as a place where "they have good schools, and you are going to one of them." At first Ernesto was afraid of the school building, which had a shingled roof rather than the red tile he had been used to in Mexico; but he felt better when he saw that all the signs at the school were in both Spanish and English. Miss Ryan, his teacher, spent most of the class time teaching her diverse bunch of first-graders the intricacies of the English language. Ernesto had never been prouder than the day Miss Ryan announced to the class that he had learned how to pronounce the word "butterfly." He learned other kinds of lessons too. Fortunately for Ernesto, at this school

> Making us into Americans did not mean scrubbing away what made us originally foreign. The teachers called us as our parents did, or as close as they could pronounce our names in Spanish or Japanese. No one was ever scolded or punished for speaking in his native tongue in the playground. It was easy for me to feel that

becoming a proud American did not mean feeling ashamed of being a Mexican.

Clearly the teachers at Ernesto's school went out of their way to help their immigrant students ease into their new national identities. They sponsored show-and-tell sessions where students could bring in examples of the crafts of their homelands and conducted mock elections each year so that the children could practice the citizenship they encouraged them to pursue.[37]

At least some of the Mexican, Japanese, Yugoslavian, Polish, and Irish children at this idyllic institution must have known how very unusual a school it was. A significant number of immigrant students faced much more pressure to Americanize by putting aside all vestiges of their ethnic or national backgrounds. The teachers at the Jewish Training School of Chicago required the Satt children to change their names from Hinda, Welvel, and Gutcha to Hilda, Willie, and Rose, so as not to betray their immigrant origins. This was typical of Jewish community institutions across the country, which, claiming to work for the immigrants' own benefit, oversaw an aggressive program of Americanization. "The new immigrants must be Americanized in spite of themselves, in the mode prescribed by their friends and benefactors," announced the *Jewish Messenger* in 1891.[38] In a county where anti-Semitism was on the rise, the Jewish community might have been particularly sensitive to a perceived need for immigrants to Americanize quickly. Even in this particularly charged environment, however, children sometimes made their own choices about retaining certain elements of tradition. Jewish girls enrolled in a class at a Milwaukee settlement house designed to teach them American cooking revolted when the teacher continually transgressed the traditional dietary laws that required separating meat from milk. These girls did not necessarily come from the most observant of homes, but keeping kosher was one of the ways in which many Jewish families attempted to hold on to some forms of tradition.

Even young children could recognize the conflict between retaining traditions from home and accepting a totally new culture. Ernesto Galarza listened to his adult relatives mock American manners and question such American practices as not keeping their feet on the floor when sitting down or boxing instead of bullfighting or addressing older people disrespectfully. He was comforted to know that at home, at least, "ours remained a Mexican family."[39] Still, Ernesto's Mexican family had immigrated to the United States in part to improve his chances for a better life, and even as a boy, he could see that the way to reach that goal was to Americanize. If he had not learned English fluently or had not adopted American clothes and style, he would have faced even more obstacles to success than those already in place for any immigrant child.

Discrimination at School and in Daily Life. For Ernesto, as for other immigrant children of color, racial discrimination was one of the greatest obstacles he faced. He was fortunate to attend schools where racial difference apparently played little part in his experiences, but when he looked for work he was not so lucky, and most American schools were not so open-minded. Discrimination within American education had a long history; periods of heavy immigration intensified it. When California began to provide public education after becoming a state in 1850, it excluded children of Asian background from its educational system. During the late 1870s a group of Chinese merchants petitioned the state to expand public education to include their children. They argued as taxpayers who supported public education in California without any benefits accruing to their own children. Tellingly, they petitioned for the establishment of separate schools, both as a matter of their own preference and because they knew the state would almost certainly deny school integration. As it was, the issue of educating Chinese children remained bitterly debated in California for decades. In 1885, Mary Tape was outraged that her American-born daughter Mamie was denied entrance to a San Francisco public school. She wrote bitterly to the Board of Education, "Just because she is descended of Chinese parents I guess she is more of a American than a good many of you that is going to prevent her being educated" [sic].[40] Despite a ruling in her favor, Mamie Tape was never allowed into her local school. The Board of Education set up a separate school in Chinatown for Chinese-American children. The California Supreme Court ruled that Chinese children had a legal right to education but said nothing about school integration.

At the end of the nineteenth century, racial segregation also expanded to include Mexican children, who as early as 1896 were forced to attend separate schools in states like California and Texas. The trumped-up rationales for segregating Mexicans included inadequate command of English, low standards of cleanliness, and genetic and physical inferiority. The connection to white attitudes toward African Americans was clear, especially following the infamous 1896 Supreme Court case *Plessy v. Ferguson*, which legitimized the concept of "separate but equal."

In San Francisco the school segregation issue came to a head after the 1906 earthquake destroyed the section of the city in which most of the Japanese lived, forcing them into other areas. To prevent Japanese students from attending regular public schools, the Board of Education ordered all Japanese, Korean, and Chinese children to attend a separate school. The Board claimed that Japanese students were too old and disruptive and therefore had to attend the segregated school in Chinatown. In fact there were only ninety-three Japanese students in question, twenty-five of them American-born citizens and only thirty-two older than fifteen.[41] The furor over this San Francisco action brought anti-Japanese sentiment to national attention, especially when President Theodore Roosevelt denounced the move and ordered it rescinded as part of U.S. treaty obligations toward Japan.

Proponents of integrated schools pointed out that Americanization could best take place in so-called mixed environments. They warned that segregated schools for Mexican or Chinese children in the Southwest were not achieving the same kinds of Americanization results as urban schools in the Northeast and Midwest that enrolled children of many backgrounds. Not everyone agreed. The eugenics expert Albert Schultz argued in his popular 1908 book *Race or Mongrel?* that

> The opinion is advanced that the public schools change the children of all races into Americans. Put a Scandinavian, a German, and Magyar boy in at one end, and they will come out Americans at the other end. Which is like saying, let a pointer, a setter, and pug enter one end of a tunnel and they will come out three greyhounds at the other end.[42]

With this kind of prejudice directed against European immigrants, it is not surprising that "nonwhite" immigrant children suffered even greater opprobrium, even before going to school.

With the exception of Roosevelt's intervention in 1906, little official help was forthcoming in immigrants' battles against school discrimination. In 1909 state representative Grove Johnson delivered a speech to the California legislature on the "Sexual Dangers of School Integration." The well-received remarks denied that Roosevelt had understood the situation and insisted he had made the wrong decision. "I am responsible," Johnson said, "to the mothers and fathers of Sacramento County who have their little daughters sitting side by side in the school rooms with matured Japs, with their base minds, their lascivious thoughts multiplied by their race and strengthened by their mode of life."[43] This diatribe, with sexualized overtones reminiscent of the rhetoric surrounding the lynching of African Americans during the same period, demonstrated the continuing power of racism to defeat logic or justice.

If anything, racism in the United States expanded during the early twentieth century. After restrictive immigration legislation took effect in the 1920s, the U.S. government listed incoming Mexicans as white to allow for sorely needed labor immigration, but in practice Mexicans were rarely seen as white. Hostility toward them remained blatant even in official venues. In a 1928 speech to the House of Representatives, Texas congressman John Box declared baldly, "Every reason which calls for the exclusion of the most wretched, ignorant, dirty, diseased, and degraded people of Europe or Asia demands that the illiterate, unclean, peonized masses moving this way from Mexico be stopped at the border."[44] A special census conducted in Los Angeles in 1927 categorized Mexicans as "red," noting that 1,790 Los Angeles schoolchildren were "red."[45] That same year the Supreme Court decided in *Lum v. Rice* that Martha Lum, of Chinese descent, could be prevented from attending a white school in Mississippi since there was a nearby "colored" school she could go to instead. The decision cited *Plessy v. Ferguson* as a precedent and held that the Mississippi constitution "divided the educable children into those of the pure white of Caucasian race, on the one hand, and the brown, yellow, and black races on the other."[46]

The institutionalized discrimination in education that affected so many immigrant children's opportunities also shaped their personal experiences. Yoshito Kawachi found that

> during recess the white children all gathered round me and bullied me, calling out "Jap! Jap!" I got to the point where I couldn't stand it anymore, so I bought candy and gave it out little by little to those who were friendly. After a while, everybody started shaking hands with me—all except two girls who persisted in being hard on me. Finally my patience broke and I hit them one day.[47]

As the most physically distinct, Asian children suffered most. Mary Paik and her brother Meung faced the taunts of their mining-town classmates, who chanted "Ching Chong, Chinaman" at them even though they were Korean.[48] Discrimination by their classmates— and sometimes their teachers too—became routine for immigrant students. When Mary Nagao went to school in California during the 1920s, the other students forced Mexican and Japanese children to sit at the back of the room and stand at the end of the cafeteria line. The teachers did not interfere and even looked the other way when these children received out-of-date textbooks and were denied access to sports equipment.

Despite obstacles of poverty and prejudice, many immigrant children succeeded in school. They enrolled in schools at approximately the same rate as American children. Their success sometimes triggered another wave of prejudice, particularly in schools with mixed populations. At San Francisco's Washington Grammar School in 1905, the four top students, all Chinese, were accused of cheating on tests by exchanging answers in Chinese. They were separated for the next test but still earned the highest scores. The Board of Education, the same body involved in the school segregation crisis the next year, rewarded this achievement by removing all four boys from the school. Similarly, when a New England elementary school chose to award its top two graduation prizes to a Jewish boy and a German girl, some parents protested against both awards going to foreigners. The parent group forced the school to give a new test. The children were vindicated as the same two students earned the top spots again.

With parents openly urging discriminatory practices, it is hardly surprising that children developed prejudices of their own at early ages. Ruth Dahl grew up in North Dakota hearing that "a Norwegian is a Swede with his brains knocked out."[49] Bruno Lasker's 1929 book *Race Attitudes in Children* found racial epithets and ethnic slurs to be common even among young children. Lasker cited the example of George, a four-year-old Syrian boy who called any child he was mad at a "Wop" because he knew it to be an insulting term.[50] Such young children learned these derogatory terms at home, but they took the attitudes so learned onto the street. In Chicago, Swedish girls called Sicilians names and did not let them play in Seward Park; Irish and Swedish boys fought Sicilian boys on the neighborhood streets.

Settlement houses, typically located in immigrant neighborhoods, tried to mediate these exchanges by bringing together mixed groups of children from their neighborhoods. The West Side House in Denver served German, Irish, and Scandinavian communities while Bethlehem Institute in Los Angeles served Russian, Japanese, Mexican, Armenian, Syrian, Italian, and Jewish populations. This strategy was part of reformers' larger push to move preexisting attitudes and impulses in a more positive direction, such as encouraging groups of boys to join the Boy Scouts or the Young Men's Christian Association (YMCA) rather than gangs. But settlement workers found it difficult to change children's minds about one another's origins. Coming from families that often viewed unfamiliar ethnic groups with deep suspicion, immigrant children eyed each other warily. Prejudice had many forms, as one settlement worker discovered when he tried to settle a conflict between children of different backgrounds.

> A Jewish gang and an Italian gang were always "at war." Finally one of the settlement workers took the two leaders by the nape of the neck and said, "Would your two gangs ever join in anything?" One of the gang leaders promptly replied: "Sure—in fightn' niggers."[51]

This unified commitment to fighting a common enemy was scarcely what the settlement worker was hoping to achieve, though it did underline the racial hierarchies at work in turn-of-the-century American life.

Learning How to Live

Not every interaction between children of different backgrounds was so negative. Immigrant children dealt with so many of the same issues, from poverty to living conditions to prejudice, that they did find common ground. As reformers and educators hoped, schools, settlement houses, organized playgrounds, and other public spaces that attracted a range of people helped homogenize childhood experiences to some degree. When children identified with one another rather than with their families, a typical consequence of successful Americanization, they preferred to spend time in one another's company. Immigrant parents, of course, could see what was happening. Some welcomed the distance that life in the United States was placing between them and their children as a necessary sacrifice to ensure a better life for the next generation. Others, however, bemoaned the dissipation of traditional family values and wondered if they had made the right decision in sharing their children's upbringing with teachers, peers, and other nonfamily members.

Shared Experiences. At school, work, and play, immigrant children interacted with one another constantly. Daily contact had a way of softening prejudices. Angelo Pelligrini and his Jewish school friend and spelling bee competitor practiced English pronunciation as they walked to and from school in the neighborhood where they both lived. In Benton County, Minnesota, a group of Swedish girls practicing folk dances asked a newly arrived French girl to teach them one of her dances. In Hawaii the diverse ethnic and racial labor force led inevitably to cultural mixing. Japanese and Portuguese children exchanged lunches at school, trading sushi for sweet buns. Pietro Campolongo worked as a "Shabbos goy" for his Jewish neighbors, lighting fires and doing other tasks forbidden to them when they observed the Sabbath on Friday nights and Saturdays. Bill Hosokawa enjoyed the company of his Jewish classmates in Seattle, and he was particularly appreciative that there were so many Jewish students in his school that the teachers did not bother to hold class on the High Holidays in the fall. Mingling with children of other backgrounds could thus lead to a widening of cultural and social horizons.

What many immigrant children shared was an abiding desire to be Americans. In a 1906 article in *The Outlook*, the educator John Foster Carr noted with some amusement that Italian children on the street seemed not at all interested in Italian games like *mora* (a guessing game) or *Lung a Tela* (a jump-rope rhyme). No, they preferred to play marbles or sing "London Bridge Is Falling Down," games they identified as American.[52] Harry Roskolenko, who grew up on New York's Lower East Side in the 1910s, recalled that all the children on Cherry Street, proud that George Washington had once lived there, reenacted American history. As he explained, "It was our way of acting out American history in fact and in legend—as new Americans!"[53] This was a ritual of Americanization that all the children on the block, whether Jewish or Italian or Polish, could share. Scouting also appealed to children across ethnic backgrounds as another path to Americanization. In San Francisco a Chinese boy scout troop formed in 1914, and there was already a Greek troop in New York. A Japanese boy scout at a California parade took his identity as an American so seriously that he publicly rebuked a native-born white man for not removing his hat as the American flag passed by.

Even when they were not consciously setting out to demonstrate their American identity, children seemed to know instinctively that just by spending a lot of time with mixed groups of peers, they were forging an identity separate from their parents and ethnic backgrounds. As a child, Sicilian Jerre Mangione played with Polish Tony Long, Jewish Abe Rappaport, and Italian Robert di Nella, even though their parents had little to do with one another. The four hundred newsboys in Cincinnati in 1908, of whom more than half were under the legal working age of fourteen, included eighty-six Germans, thirty-six Jews, twenty-five Irish, five Italians, three English, three Dutch, two Hungarians, and one Indian. It was in their best interests to cooperate with one another regardless of how their families and communities might get along.[54] The city streets offered multiple opportunities to cross cultural boundaries, from employment such as the newsboys found to an abundance of exotic foods. For very little money, Greek children could buy pickles, herring, and chickpeas and acquire a taste for these eastern European foods while their Jewish counterparts experimented with baklava and moussaka. All immigrant children tasted American treats such as taffy apples, watermelon, and ice cream. The street became a microcosm of their exposure to other cultures.

City children conducted their own social lives in an environment in which there was nowhere to play but on the stoops and sidewalks and fire escapes of the street. Tenements took up whole lots, with front, middle, and rear houses huddled together and sheds, coal bins, and stables occupying any other spaces. With such limited space, children had to be creative. When Anthony Dicristo was growing up in the heavily Italian and Sicilian Third Ward in Milwaukee, few children owned store-bought toys, but they invented their own playthings. Boys made a "push" by attaching a board and wheels to the bottom of a peach box and pushing one another around the neighborhood. In Pittsburgh's Boone Alley, a thoroughfare thirty feet wide and paved with cement cobblestones, children played baseball in summer, football and soccer in fall, and basketball between seasons. They used whatever came to hand as bases, from beaten-up derby hats to discarded corsets. Enforcing the rules of these American games was more important than enforcing rules about which groups could or could not play them. No one monitored what kind of children jumped into New York's East Broadway fountain on hot summer days except the police, who chased them all out regardless of background. Although there were certainly ethnic gangs and urban territories, children often mixed indiscriminately in their street play.

The distinction that played some role on the street was gender, not national origin. While boys played marbles and leapfrog in the middle of the street, girls jumped rope and played with balls on the steps and stoops. They looked after babies and toddlers, a responsibility boys rarely had. Girls who transgressed gender boundaries might be admired by some of their male peers, but they were likely to get in trouble with their families. Kate Simon received a lecture from her father for not remembering her proper place on the streets of her Bronx neighborhood.

> I was always in the street running wild with the Italian and Polish beasts. I didn't take proper care of my brother, I climbed with boys, I ran with boys, I skated with them on far streets. Mr. Kaplan had seen me and told [my father]. And how would this life, this playing with boys, end? I would surely become a street girl, a prostitute, and wind up being shipped to a filthy diseased brothel crawling with hairy tropical bugs, in Buenos Aires.[55]

Kate was not sure what a brothel was, other than an undesirable location, but she wanted to avoid a beating and thus became more discreet about playing with the boys in the middle of the street. Any of the girls in her neighborhood—Italian, Polish, Greek, or Jewish like her—had to engage in similar subterfuge to avoid their prescribed space on the sidelines. Not all play was gender segregated, however. An 1896 study of almost two thousand children in Worcester, Massachusetts, found that among children nine to fifteen years of age, five of the favorite ten games were named by both boys and girls, all of whom enjoyed sledding, skating, and playing ball, tag, and hide-and-seek.[56]

Reformers saw the chaos of the city streets as an invitation to intervene and improve the lives of immigrant children by organizing

Immigrant children playing on the roof garden of the Washington School in Boston, 1909. Playground reformers believed that supervised play would develop children's moral character. *(Library of Congress)*

their play. From 1880 to 1920, municipal governments spent more than a hundred million dollars on organized playgrounds. The Playground Association of America, founded in 1906, set out to bring children's play under professional supervision and to encourage certain kinds of socialization seen as integral to Americanization, especially teamwork. Most municipal playgrounds offered younger children equipment such as sandboxes, slides, swings, and seesaws but reserved their largest spaces for older children's team games, like football and baseball, in order to encourage organized play and cooperative effort. As with many Progressive Era reform efforts, both the motives and the success of playground reform were mixed. The Playground Association of America undoubtedly helped provide funding for public spaces that benefited children with limited access to any kind of open space. The playgrounds offered equipment and sports that otherwise would have been out of immigrant children's reach. But some immigrant parents viewed playgrounds with suspicion as sites of idleness, and there was never enough room for all the children in a given area to play. The team sports that playground reformers hoped would inculcate American sportsmanship and team mentality were not usually open to girls and could backfire by reinforcing ethnic loyalties. As with other forms of Americanization efforts, reformers tended to underestimate many children's interest in holding on to at least some of their traditions and culture.

Family Values. The only way reformers would have been able to better guarantee Americanization would have been to remove immigrant children from their families altogether. Children might play on the street, visit the playground, and go to school in diverse groups, but then most of them went home, where they belonged to a different kind of community in which their parents were the authority figures. Immigrant parents tried hard to sustain their children's family loyalties, replicating the economic unit of the household with an affective unit bound by emotional ties and shared values. Although the specifics varied depending on ethnic or national origin, children played an important part in the development of immigrant family values. Issei poems that confessed, "Working together / Making effort faithfully / Till they all grow up," or "Alien hardships / Made bearable by the hope / I hold for my children," probably expressed feelings held by most immigrant parents.[57] Their idea of success revolved around their children as both symbols and real people.

As real people, immigrant children learned early on about the values of their families and communities. Japanese children heard constantly about *on*, a permanent obligation of respect for parents; *gaman*, perseverance; *ninjo*, empathy and sensitivity; and *enryo*, modesty and humility. They also learned that it was preferable to avoid direct conflict within the family and outside it. Given the contrast between ethnic family values and some elements of American values, it is not surprising that many different groups shared a commitment to trying to minimize generational conflict if at all possible. *El Regidor*, a San Antonio newspaper, advised Mexican girls to "be obedient to your parents to the point where they need not tell you anything through their lips but through their eyes." The periodical went on to offer even more practical advice: "If you have any talent, hide it."[58] Only then could Mexican girls live in harmony with their families.

The problem, of course, was that in an American ethos of individualism, suggesting that immigrant children hide their individual abilities, or subordinate them to the community, left them with extremely mixed messages. The conflict was visible across cultures. Italian parents brought with them the idea that "*Una mazza, lavero e pane fanno figli belli*"—"A cane, work, and bread make fine children." This set of values, accompanied by the idea that children should be *ben educato*, well educated, but not necessarily in the sense of formal schooling, left Italian children struggling to reconcile the competing demands of home, school, and work.[59]

The stakes were high for immigrant parents who hoped to achieve success through their children but were ambivalent about the American path toward success. Parents knew there was a darker side to their children's achievement, since success in America was often defined or enabled by abandoning "foreign" traditions. Chinese immigrants referred to their children as *t'oa jee doy*, those who were ignorant of Chinese culture, or *chok sing*, bamboo poles. They lamented the fact that their children were as hollow as bamboo, empty of tradition. Like Chinese families, immigrants of all backgrounds took steps to ensure that their old worlds would not be immediately forgotten in their new world.

Resisting Americanization

When children went home from school and play at the end of the day, they returned to ethnic environments and specific cultural activities. On the streets Polish boys played ball games with their mixed peer group, but at home they played *klipa*, a Polish game that involved balancing and picking up four- to eight-inch sticks. At school Japanese girls learned about Betsy Ross alongside their classmates, but at home they heard Japanese fairy tales about Momotaro the Peach Boy and the Tongue-Cut Sparrow. Immigrant children lived in two worlds, the heterogeneous world of the peers they met at school, work, and play, and the homogeneous world of their families. As strong as the pressure to Americanize was in the former, it was almost always balanced by a concern with maintaining at least some cultural traditions in the latter. Immigrant communities deployed two major strategies to preserve cultural continuity. One was the creation of schools to ensure that children would learn the language, customs, and traditions of their ethnic heritage; the other was the celebration of family events and holidays within the ethnic community. Language schools were found in virtually every immigrant community in the United States during the period of mass immigration. These schools bore a responsibility secondary only to (and in some cases greater than) the home in preserving traditional culture. They played an important role in immigrant children's lives regardless of their ethnic background or country of origin. Family and communal activities also reinforced children's allegiance to their traditions. Many immigrants lived close to relatives and saw them often. They grew up and celebrated holidays within tight ethnic communities. All of these ethnic events served the purposes of both maintaining traditional culture and keeping parents and children connected to each other despite the ever-widening gaps in experience that separated them.

Language Schools. Immigrant parents and institutions had a number of reasons for supporting language schools. On the most basic level, parents feared, with a great deal of justification, that a language gap between them and their children would result in other kinds of gaps. One Italian mother in Boston pleaded, "Please don't send my children to an *American school,* for as soon as they learn English they will not be my children anymore."[60] In Cleveland, even those Syrian immigrant parents who had learned English themselves spoke only Syrian at home so that "their children may not get away from them."[61] Immigrants also resented the interference of state and society in family relationships as represented by the literal lack of communication between parents and children who did not speak the same language. Early in the period of mass immigration, local communities often succeeded in passing laws to require children to attend schools with instruction in English. In 1890 such laws passed in Wisconsin and Illinois, aimed primarily at German immigrants, but they met stiff resistance and were eventually repealed. Writing in 1925 about a successful legal challenge to an Oregon bill that would have required all children to attend public schools and be taught in English, a Croatian priest noted, "In America parents have priority over the state when it comes to their children. Parents raise their children and therefore their rights with regard to children come before the rights of the government."[62] If immigrant parents wanted their children to learn the language of their ancestry and homeland, they could and would provide the opportunity to do so in language schools.

Three major categories of language schools were available in turn-of-the-century America: parochial or church schools, nationalist schools, and culture or heritage schools. All provided immigrant children with language instruction and often a great deal more. These categories were never entirely distinct. Even language schools focused primarily on nationalism, for example, were often sponsored by or housed in churches. But the three kinds of institutions

reflected the variety of roles that language schools played within immigrant communities across cultures and across the country.

Parochial schools were among the most common providers of
language instruction to Catholic immigrant children. The Catholic
church was intensely concerned about the issue of children's religious instruction in Protestant America. In 1884 the American
church hierarchy commanded Catholic parents to send their children to parochial schools, altering charters so that nuns could teach
boys as well as girls. As Bishop John Scalabrini explained in a letter
to the future Pope Pius X, "a very apt element in the preservation of
the faith is exactly the preservation of the language of origin."[63] Because the church had recommended in the 1891 Lucerne Memorial
that parishes be organized and staffed according to nationality, it
followed that parochial schools would offer instruction in the native
languages of their constituencies. At the turn of the century, for example, nearly half the parochial schools in New England were dominated by French Canadians to the extent that all subjects were
taught in French. Of the twenty-three parish schools in Detroit by
1900, six were Polish. In the Polish parochial schools, Polish was the
language of instruction for catechism, Bible history, poetry, church
history, literature, Polish history, art, and music. For older children,
English was used for those subjects deemed less important, including geography and nature study. These schools were particularly important to Polish Catholics in America because they offered Polish
immigrants a way to stake a claim to a church dominated by Irish
and German Catholics.

Not every Catholic group linked ethnic parishes to ethnic
parochial schools. In 1900 only 37 percent of Catholic communities
in America supported their own parochial schools.[64] Among ten
Italian parishes in Chicago in 1910 there was only one Italian parochial school, and in Detroit there was still only one Italian parochial school by the mid-1920s. More than seven times as many Italian children in New York went to public school as attended

parochial school. These statistics may reflect the much-lamented anti-clericalism of Italian Catholics.[65]

Other factors could also affect the likelihood of children attending ethnic parochial schools. In Pittsburgh before World War I, the First Catholic Slovak Union encouraged its members to send their children to Slovak parochial schools where both Catholicism and the Slovak language could be maintained. But schools were rarely incorporated into church building plans, and it was difficult to raise funds for separate school construction. As a result, in 1914 there was just one Slovak parochial school in Pittsburgh.

Other religious groups also supported full-day schools. Those sponsored by the Armenian Apostolic church taught Armenian children language and customs, and local Lutheran churches conducted "vacation schools" to teach Swedish children church history, catechism, and Swedish. The folk high school movement, initiated in Denmark, appeared in the United States as well, and Danish children and adolescents learned traditional subjects and Danish in churches across the Midwest. In some Indiana towns, Dutch Calvinists established Christian day schools which through the 1930s continued to enroll more Dutch children than the county public schools. Greek schools were typically also supported by the church. In a handful of Greek day schools in the United States before World War I, all subjects were taught in Greek and the educational concentration was on Greek Orthodoxy and Greek history. Only the Greek Orthodox church could sustain these language schools, which were expensive to run and difficult to staff. While these religiously sponsored language schools lacked the overwhelming institutional support of the Catholic parochial schools, they nevertheless played an important role in preserving ethnic heritage and culture. The Massachusetts Immigration Commission reported that by 1917 there were more than ninety bilingual schools in the state offering half a day of instruction in English and half a day of mostly religious instruction in Polish, Italian, French, or Greek.[66]

Nationalism supplied another motivation for immigrant parents to send their children to language schools. In an 1899 "America Letter," an immigrant reminded his Czech compatriots to speak Slovak at home and send their children to a Slovak school, "for the hope of each nation lies in its youth, and if they forget their mother tongue, they will forget their nationality."[67] In 1918 the Czech-American Central School Association urged Czech parents to make sure their children had "a foundation in the history of the Czech people" so they would "love that nation, adhere to its ways, and proudly acclaim allegiance to it."[68] The language schools that Korean children attended celebrated Korean independence meetings each March 1 with student presentations and orations in Korean. Among "The Eleven National Commandments Aimed at Instilling a Modern National Consciousness" published in the Ukrainian periodical *Svoboda* in 1914 was the injunction that "The Ukrainian child should associate exclusively with Ukrainian children and speak only in Ukrainian when in their company."[69] Ukrainian schools such as St. Basil's in Philadelphia provided the space to accomplish these nationalist goals, though it proved unrealistic to expect Ukrainian children to spend time only with one another.

The issue of nationalism could divide as well as unite ethnic groups committed to maintaining language schools. Jewish education, for instance, encompassed an array of schools in which the language of instruction revealed the divergent goals of the educators. Most Jewish children received religious education in supplementary classes after their regular public school day was over. Jewish parents of a Zionist bent in New York might choose to send their children, girls and boys, to the developing system of Talmud Torah schools, where the concentration was on Hebrew. More traditional parents might send their sons to a *cheder* where the Bible and Talmud were studied under the guidance of Yiddish-speaking teachers. More liberal Jews might decide on Sabbath schools that offered limited training in the Hebrew language but provided other religious subjects in English. The somewhat anomalous position of Judaism as both religion and ethnicity contributed to this wide variety of Jewish language schools.

More numerous than either religious or nationalist language schools were the culture or heritage language schools, though it would be impossible to draw impermeable boundaries around any of these categories. In Waterville, Maine, for instance, the three hundred Syrians who settled there during the 1920s arranged for the more literate immigrants among them to teach Arabic to their children in private homes. Larger immigrant communities organized networks of heritage schools. By 1913 most sizable Ukrainian communities had heritage schools in place. A sufficient number of these Ukrainian heritage schools existed that an organization called the *Ridna Shkola* began in 1927 to standardize teacher training, curricula, and tests. In 1912 a San Francisco conference sponsored by the Japanese Association of America resolved that the main purpose of language schools was to teach future permanent residents of the United States, as opposed to children who would eventually return to Japan. To that end, Japanese language and cultural instruction was vital for every Japanese child but would remain supplemental to "American education." At a subsequent conference, the newly formed Japanese Teachers Association of America agreed that the basic subjects of language schools would be Japanese language, history, and geography, through which moral education would also be taught.

As illustrated by the centralization of the Japanese Teachers Association of America, Asian immigrants sustained some of the most viable and long-lived culture and heritage schools in America. The first Korean immigrants to arrive in Hawaii, just after 1900, immediately established language schools to teach their children Korean language, values, customs, history, and geography. Between 1907 and 1940, 18 Korean language schools were founded in Hawaii alone. In 1931, 10 schools had 520 students.[70] Like these Korean schools, most culture and heritage schools met after public school. Chinese language schools typically met from 4 or 5 p.m. to 7 or 8 p.m. four or five days a week, plus Saturdays from 9 a.m. to 1 p.m. By the late 1920s there were 56 Chinese language schools for elementary and high school students in the United States.[71] Pardee Lowe spent his late afternoon hours at Master Wang's Institute, first learning basic Chinese language, history, geography, and philosophy, then practicing writing Chinese characters. The school that Jade Snow Wong attended as a child taught 20 to 30 students Chinese calligraphy, poetry, philosophy, literature, history, correspondence, and religion. Her parents expected her to do her Chinese homework before her American homework.

Neither Pardee nor Jade found language school particularly interesting or enjoyable. Pardee complained, "It was obvious that this Chinese curriculum was not entirely understood or wanted by the students. The mass of material hurled at us daily proved indigestible."[72] Jade learned the manners of a Chinese lady—to be "trouble-free, unobtrusive, quiescent, cooperative"—but little else.[73] Pardee eventually went to another language school, where for a tuition fee of five dollars a month he was taught very formal Chinese language and philosophy. In high school he convinced his father that it was impossible for him to do well at both American high school and Chinese school simultaneously. He stopped attending language school and did not really learn Chinese well until he went to Stanford years later.

Students in Japanese language schools had similar experiences, and there were large numbers of Japanese schools and students. One study of Nisei men showed that more than 85 percent of them had attended language schools as children.[74] Each school was run by a local board of trustees responsible for hiring teachers, planning policy, and overseeing finances. In larger schools tuition fees covered the costs, but in smaller schools everyone in the Japanese community was expected to contribute. Classes usually met twice a

Female students at a Japanese language school in Portland, Oregon, circa 1929. The principal and his wife sit at the center. Note the wide age range. *(University of Washington Libraries)*

week in the late afternoons, with teachers paid from $55 to $200 a month. Despite these attempts at organization and efforts to involve whole families through ceremonies and meetings, the schools were usually unsuccessful in teaching Japanese to the students. One former student explained that "motivation to learn was not very high" among students who were teased by their public school classmates for being Japanese.[75] The language schools may have been more successful at teaching the conduct expected of Japanese children. One girl recalled that at her American school she was "a jumping, screaming, roustabout Yankee," but at her Japanese school she "suddenly became a modest, faltering, earnest little Japanese girl with a small, timid voice."[76]

Christian missionaries quickly adapted the idea of language schools to their own goals. During the late 1890s, Protestant missionaries successfully ran the Sokabe Boarding School in Hawaii for the children of Buddhist parents. The students learned American manners by living at the school and studying regular school subjects. But the Sokabe Boarding School also offered Japanese language, literature, and history twice a week, a feature of the curriculum that made the school appealing to parents otherwise put off by the twice daily Bible readings and the custom of saying grace before meals. The missionary effort succeeded because the school did not insist that the children cut all ties to their heritage in the process of becoming good Christians and good Americans. Welsh Congregationalists had a similar goal in mind when they included a special section for children in *Y Cenhadwr Americanaidd* (*The American Missionary*), a religious magazine published from 1840 to 1901. They believed that language could function as a bridge between immigrant parents and their children rather than as an insurmountable barrier. Everyone involved in these endeavors, from teachers and writers to immigrant parents and children themselves, also believed it inevitable that children's primary language in America would be English.

Although language schools were common features of immigrant children's experiences, parents as well as students viewed them with some ambivalence. A Lithuanian man during the early 1900s explained that he had no plans to send his American-born son to a Lithuanian Catholic school conducted in two small rooms by two Lithuanian priests. He preferred to send him to an American school with unionized teachers. It was also the case that some children moved easily between public and parochial schools. Polish children in Buffalo might go to a Polish parochial school until their First Communion, then to a public school for the rest of their education. The parochial schools themselves encouraged this pattern when the demand for enrollment was high. In Buffalo the parish priests sometimes advanced the dates of First Communions to move one class out and allow another into the parochial school, thinking it best to teach as many students as possible Polish and religious subjects before their parents lost interest.

At public schools with large immigrant populations, significant numbers of students went to language schools after dismissal. More progressive school districts even allowed language schools to operate in public school facilities. In Los Angeles the school board granted Russian, Italian, French, and Jewish groups permission to offer language instruction to students after school hours. Ironically, widespread attendance at the various kinds of language schools gave immigrant children of all backgrounds a set of common experiences at the same time it strengthened their diverse sets of ethnic and religious traditions. The Jewish students at Talmud Torah classes might have been learning very different things from what their Greek classmates were learning at their churches, but they shared the experience of exposure to their heritage. As institutions, language schools were an example of the critical social tasks assigned to education at the turn of the century. Whether offering a combination of language and religious education or a focus on ethnicity and nationalism, language schools helped immigrant families come to terms with the demands of Americanization.

Holidays. From children's perspective, holidays and other ritual events were probably more successful than language schools at preserving both ethnic/religious and family ties. Holiday celebrations provided important opportunities for children and adults to interact in ethnic settings. On holidays and festive occasions, children stayed up as late as they wanted since they were full members of the celebrating community. One Italian child remembered that during communal celebrations, each child would be picked up and put to bed as he or she dozed off, waking up the next morning in a row of children on the grandparents' bed. The festive spirit and the relaxation of rules kept children interested in their family and community and gave them an attachment to their ethnic, religious, or national backgrounds, cemented in fond childhood memories.

Holidays were both secular and religious in nature. Numerous immigrant groups sustained an abiding attachment to their home-lands and expressed their loyalties by continuing to celebrate important national occasions. For example, in 1893, Danish immi-grants from South Jutland, then occupied by Prussia, met in San Francisco's Woodward Gardens on June 5 to celebrate Constitution Day. They saluted Danish flags, sang Danish songs, and delivered orations on behalf of their homeland. Few of these immigrants had any intention of returning to South Jutland, but they believed it important to teach their children about their national heritage. Similarly, to make sure their children would develop ties to their country of origin, one Norwegian farm family papered the inside walls of their sod house with Norwegian newspapers. On May 17, Norwegian Independence Day (*syttende mai*), they commemorated the signing of the 1814 Norwegian constitution. These communal celebrations helped alleviate Norwegian farmers' isolation on the prairies and were also sponsored by urban branches of the Norwe-gian National League in Chicago, New York, and elsewhere. Com-munity organizers made sure to include children in the folk festivals associated with May 17, often by organizing special parades for them. Immigrant children learned that they could retain and even celebrate their national origins in their new national setting. After all, as one Danish festival participant wrote gratefully, "Here in America there is no law against loving the language and memories of our land."[77] These celebrations of national origin helped children learn how to blend their traditions with American culture.

Like political nationalism, communal solidarity inspired holi-days and celebrations. On St. Nicholas' Day in Scotch Plains, New Jersey, all the local Italian families staged a parade and held races and fireworks to raise money for the St. Nicholas Society. On St. Basil's Day, Greek children visited the Greek stores in their neighborhoods to wish their compatriots good luck in business. The continuing importance of ethnic culture led to simultaneous celebration of religion and ethnicity.

Even religious holidays that otherwise reached across national backgrounds were often observed within particular ethnic settings. Polish children knew they were not alone in celebrating Assumption Day on August 15, yet their activities on that day differed from those of other Catholic celebrants. They took flowers, apples, and carrots to the Polish churches for blessings, later drying out the bouquets to be used as ornaments. The church was the center of all Polish communal activities. As one boy put it, "Church was almost a second home to us. I mean we never miss[ed] a novena or any service at all."[78] Other groups had similar rituals to bind home, church, and community together for children. A day or two before Christmas, *El Agüelo* (the grandfather) visited Mexican children at home, toting a large bag of gifts of cookies and candy—and to use to carry bad children away with him. When *El Agüelo* came, the children recited prayers and then danced in a circle with him. Such child-centered rituals provided immigrant children with strong emotional connections to their communities and families.

Christmas in particular afforded opportunities for other kinds of holiday celebrations. "No matter how poor you were," said one Italian boy, "you always had a Christmas."[79] Not all Christmas traditions were in fact religious in nature. Growing up on the mining frontier, Bruna Pieracci recalled that "we did not learn until our early teens that Christmas day was the birthday of the Christ child." What they did learn was that Christmas was a time to expect a gift of an orange or apple from the mine owner and the family ritual of hanging brightly colored stockings for the small gifts their impoverished parents could provide.[80] Children in public schools, irrespective of their backgrounds, usually celebrated Christmas by participating in some kind of pageant or program and then receiving a bag of candy or piece of fruit. Gift giving and receiving were the common denominator of Christmas celebrations, regardless of the particular religious niceties observed by various immigrant groups. Norwegian farm children, who decorated poplar trees because they had no access to fir trees on the prairie, enjoyed their Christmas pork roast and then went *Yulebekking*, putting on masks and funny clothes to visit neighbors' homes and collect gifts from them. God and church played little part in this ritual.

The centrality of holiday celebrations placed some immigrant children under enormous pressure. Mary Paik's family was both Christian and poor, which made Christmas a trial in a mining camp with few churches and no other Christian Korean families. The Paiks could not even afford the not particularly religious symbol of a tree, so two weeks after Christmas, Mary and her brother scavenged for the best tree put out as garbage and brought it home to decorate. For non-Christian children, Christmas could be nightmarish, an open symbol of their difference at a time of year when Christmas theoretically reached across all boundaries to embrace the world in Christian benevolence. To counter these negative feelings, certain immigrant groups relied on other kinds of holidays to bring tradition alive for their children. Chinese immigrants in America celebrated *Qing Ming*, the Pure Brightness Festival, in the spring, honoring the memorial day by visiting Chinese cemeteries. They also celebrated the fall Moon Festival, a day that had traditionally marked a thanksgiving for good harvests. What Chinese children in America looked forward to most, though, was the Chinese New Year. Twenty-four hours before the New Year, celebrated in January or February depending on the alignment of the Chinese and Western calendars, women swept their houses and warned their children to avoid vulgar or profane language. They would not sweep again until after the New Year lest they sweep away their good luck. Children shot off firecrackers to scare away evil spirits. They exchanged *lay shee*, good-luck packages of silver wrapped in red paper.

Five boys at a New Year's celebration in New York's Chinatown in 1911. Note the combination of traditional and Western dress. *(Library of Congress)*

The Japanese New Year was similarly festive. The Japanese arranged three kinds of trees outside their doors and held parties where the children learned to play *karuta*, a card game, and *sugoroku*, Japanese backgammon. Japanese children celebrated other nonreligious holidays as well, most notably Girl's Day on March 3 and Boy's Day on May 5. On Girl's Day, or Doll Festival Day, girls set out rows of dolls representing characters from Japanese history and literature. They put out food for the dolls, dressed up, and visited their friends' doll displays. On Boy's Day, or the Festival of Flags, boys hung out paper carps on fishing rods. They displayed solider and hero figures with weapons and fought mock battles. In stark contrast to the individualism of American birthdays, Girl's and Boy's Days served as community-wide celebrations of birth and children.

The syncretizing of traditional religious values with the Americanizing forces of public values led to compromises, cultural blends, and new forms of celebration. At the turn of the century, thousands of Jewish children participated each year in school Christmas pageants, though many of their parents told them not to sing the words to the carols. In a neat twist of civic culture against itself, in 1916 Boston Jewish community leaders used the First Amendment as justification for their complaint that Jewish children should not be forced to sing Christmas carols in public schools. One of the main reasons for the inflation of Chanukah into a major Jewish holiday was to ward off the "December Dilemma" by giving Jewish children something from their own heritage to celebrate. In another example of ethnic communities combining elements of more than one tradition, Chinese children saw fireworks at least twice a year, at the Chinese New Year and on the Fourth of July.

Food played an important role in all these celebrations. In general, food served as an ethnic marker for immigrant families. Mothers used traditional foods to keep their children connected to their ethnic backgrounds. Italian children found, for example, that food was a major area of agreement with their parents. They were rarely embarrassed by their food, chose to eat Italian food in and out of the home, and valued traditional home cooking even if they might otherwise have been disinterested in Italian culture. Immigrant children of many backgrounds knew there would be special delicacies for each holiday and tended to remember them vividly, if not always fondly. No Norwegian festive occasion was complete without *lefse*, baked potato pancakes, *ømmegrøt*, sour cream porridge, and the either loved or reviled *lutefisk*, dried preserved cod. Pardee Lowe's mother dubbed Thanksgiving with the Chinese-sounding title of "The Festival of the Barbecued Turkey" but celebrated it with an American-style dinner.

Like holiday observances, food served some immigrant children as a bridge between cultures. A Nisei recalled that the maintenance of traditional holiday customs and the adoption of new ones was just one more symbol of his immigrant childhood.

> I sat down to American breakfasts and Japanese lunches. My palate developed a fondness for rice along with corned beef and cabbage. I said grace at mealtime in Japanese, and recited the Lord's Prayer at night in English. I hung my stockings over the fireplace at Christmas, and toasted *mochi* at Japanese New Year. . . . I was spoken to by both parents in Japanese or in English. I answered in whichever was convenient or in a curious mixture of both.[81]

The effect of such Americanization flowed in more than one direction. By the 1920s, despite the continuing tradition of Christmas concerts, Thanksgiving was the most widely celebrated holiday in the schools. Thanksgiving became intimately related to contemporary social conditions, with native-born and immigrant children alike viewing the Pilgrims as the first refugees looking for freedom and opportunity. This heightened attention to Thanksgiving, now removed from its origins as a religious or harvest festival, demonstrated the impact of immigration on public culture. Celebrating Thanksgiving as an expression of the opportunities of the New World symbolized a promise to immigrants of a better life for their children. At the same time it eased native-born Americans' fears of the foreigners among them by reminding them that their ancestors too had been immigrants. Such developments in civic culture did not solve all the problems produced by immigration, as 1920s restrictionist policies made very clear. Still, for immigrant children already coming of age in America, it seemed to be at least possible to earn acceptance and security as they moved into adolescence. These goals were more realistic for some than for others, but, as was typically the case for immigrants, the opportunity was what mattered.

CHAPTER FOUR

Adolescent Years

I know that I became a staunch American at that party. I was
with children who had been brought here from all over the
world. The fathers and mothers, like my father and mother, had
come in search of a free and happy life. And we were all having a
good time at a party as the guests of an American, Jane Addams.
We were all poor. Some of us were underfed. Some of us had
holes in our shoes. But we were not afraid of each other. . . .
While I felt that I had done nothing wrong or sinful by going to
that Christmas party, I still hesitated telling Mother where I had
been. I was glad that she did not ask me.

    —Hilda Satt Polacheck, *I Came a Stranger*[1]

☞ WHEN HILDA SATT accompanied a neighborhood friend to a
Christmas party at Chicago's Hull House in 1896, she went with
mixed emotions. Thirteen years old at the time, Hilda at first feared
that Jewish children like her might be hurt at the party, since her
experiences in Poland before her family's immigration a few years
earlier had taught her that Christmas was a dangerous time for
Jews. Reassured by her Irish friend, whom she had met while playing on South Halsted Street where they both lived, she agreed to
go. Hilda and her siblings attended the Jewish Training School of

Chicago rather than public school, and she had never been as close to a Christmas tree as she was in the settlement house party room. Instinctively she knew her mother would not approve, but she nonetheless settled in and enjoyed the company of a mixed group of peers.

Hilda did not return to Hull House for some time after her initial encounter with Jane Addams's storied settlement house. The following winter she decided to leave school, where she had completed fifth grade at age fourteen, and go to work to help support her family. Since her father had died shortly after the Satt family arrived in the United States, Hilda and her older sister provided the only income for the household. Her sister secured a job for her at the same knitting factory where she already worked. The two young women worked six days a week from 7:30 a.m. until 6:00 p.m. with a half-hour lunch break. The factory paid piecework wages so that even the fastest worker could earn no more than five dollars a week. Hilda and her co-workers, most of whom were also adolescent immigrant girls, lost pay every time a machine broke down or a needle broke. The management took the doors off the toilets so workers would not spend too much time in them. Accidents occurred regularly, leaving workers maimed, uncompensated, and unemployable.

After spending four years supporting her family by working in these conditions, Hilda became interested in union activity. As a result she was denounced as a troublemaker by a management spy and summarily fired. Then eighteen and at a loss as to what to do next, she spent a day wandering the streets of Chicago, visiting Marshall Field's, Grant Park, and the Art Institute, and then spent a week looking for work. Once she found a new job, she decided to stop by Hull House after work one day to seek out entertainment. Jane Addams immediately assigned her to work in the new Labor Museum, and Hilda began to spend all her free time at Hull House. She took classes in cross-stitch embroidery and dancing and joined a reading club. As a result of the talent Hilda displayed in a writing class, Addams helped arrange for her to take a course at the University of Chicago. In this diverse ethnic environment, Hilda thrived, learning many of the things her truncated education had not taught her. She ultimately wrote plays and taught English to the next generation of immigrant children at Hull House. When in 1912 she married William Polacheck in a ceremony in a rabbi's study, Jane Addams held a reception for her at the settlement house that Hilda credited with her transformation into a thoroughly American girl.

In many ways, Hilda's experiences as an adolescent typified those of her immigrant peers in Chicago and around the country. Economic circumstances forced her to abandon secondary schooling and go to work, yet she eventually found other means of extending her education. She fiercely wanted acceptance as a true American, even though she knew her Jewish mother would strongly prefer that the road to Americanization not pass through a room with a Christmas tree in it. In Hilda's case, family ties of love and affection managed to overcome the growing gap in language, skills, and religious customs between mother and daughter. Many other immigrant adolescents were not as fortunate, however, and their parents sometimes grew so desperate to hold on to their children that they relied on intervention by social workers and even the nascent juvenile justice system.

Hilda's sunny portrayal of her own experiences as a "Hull House girl" also overlooked the very real discrimination faced by many of her immigrant peers, especially those who appeared racially distinct to native-born Americans. Their rejection by mainstream American society and their continuing appreciation for at least some traditional customs encouraged many immigrant adolescents to settle into a heavily insular social life. They might well have friends of varying backgrounds at school or work or in the neighborhood, but they often chose to spend most of their free time with peers from the same national or ethnic background. This choice was particularly apparent when it came to courtship, dating, and marriage. Whether it was out of respect for (or fear of) their parents or a genuine desire to maintain a specific set of values and customs, the vast majority of immigrant adolescents opted for "their own kind" through the 1920s. They did so in the American context of exerting the right to choose and engaging in the newly emerging dating patterns of the early twentieth century, but they made that choice in a traditional social context. It probably never occurred to Hilda that she would marry anyone not Jewish. She had non-Jewish friends but confined her dating pool to the Jewish men who were realistic potential spouses.

Hilda did not marry as an adolescent, but many other immigrants did. For girls, especially, early marriage confirmed the gender patterns that would shape their lives. Since the social destiny of virtually all girls in America at the turn of the century, regardless of background, was presumed to be marriage and motherhood, there were few reasons to delay marriage other than economic circumstances. Sociologists have defined five key steps in the transition to adulthood: leaving school, entering the paid workforce, leaving parental homes, marrying, and establishing new households. Since immigrants were so likely to leave school and find employment during their adolescence, it is not entirely surprising that some also chose to leave parental homes and establish new households by marrying young. Girls in particular had few other options if they wished to leave home, as even the freer social codes of the 1910s and 1920s did not confer respectability on young women living alone. If immigrant girls wished to live as American women, they might have to wait until they married and set up their own households.

Gender clearly played a key role in every other life-cycle stage, but it became particularly salient for adolescence. As immigrants approached adulthood, however defined, the separation of boys and girls took on more importance. Gender could work in more than one direction in adolescents' lives. For instance, immigrant girls often found comforting consonance in the value placed on women's domestic roles in both their old and new worlds. On the other hand, immigrant boys sometimes found that the tools and skills they needed to achieve American definitions of individual masculine success in the workplace clashed with their family's traditional collective culture.

Idealized models of adolescence exerted enormous power and pressure on immigrant teenagers. They often felt that the stories of their lives in America would be irrevocably written during their youth. Gender was consistently key to their aspirations and their range of opportunities. In both structural and personal terms, gender affected immigrant youth regardless of differences in ethnic or sometimes even class backgrounds. This is not to suggest that particular ethnic identity made no difference in young people's lives, but there were striking similarities across such boundaries. Immigrant adolescents found that gender deeply influenced their experiences of education, work, Americanization, discrimination, social and family life, and interaction with the state.

A Variety of Responsibilities

Immigrant adolescents in turn-of-the-century America had several sets of responsibilities. Most were members of the working class, so their primary responsibility was to their families and households. Even more surely than younger children, adolescents had to work. Some of them came to the United States on their own and literally would have starved on the streets or in the fields if they had not immediately secured employment of some kind. Others came with their families but were just as essential to the economic welfare of their households as their parents, sometimes more so. While immigrant families of many backgrounds, living in both urban and rural areas, often hoped to provide their children with some education, in most cases this desire did not extend into adolescence. Since rela-

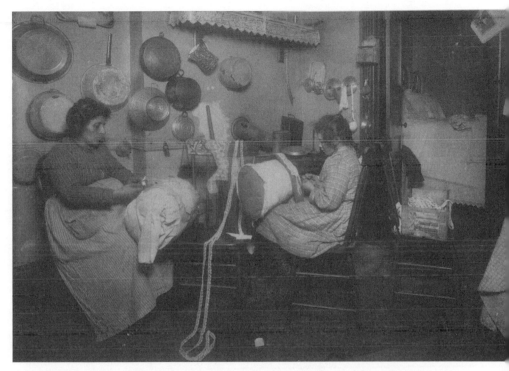

A woman and her thirteen-year-old daughter at work on pillow lace in the kitchen of their New York City tenement in 1911. Poor lighting made this painstaking labor difficult. *(Library of Congress)*

tively few American adolescents graduated from high school at the turn of the century, immigrant families merely replicated the social and economic patterns of their new world by assuming that formal secondary education was the province of the privileged few.

As new Americans, however, immigrant adolescents felt they had another responsibility, more cultural than economic in nature, and that was to realize the American dream of fulfilling their individual potential. The rampant individualism of the late 1800s and early 1900s played a role in the way they thought about themselves and their opportunities. Yes, adolescents owed their families their time and labor. But they also owed it to themselves to develop lives outside their families. If that meant making economic and personal sacrifices in order to prolong education, so be it. If that meant renegotiating relationships so that family formations would resemble the idealized "American" family, focused on the children, so be it. If that meant constant disagreement with their parents, so be it.

Education was both the cause and effect of ideas about becoming American. Adolescents who had attended elementary school absorbed ideas about what their lives would be like, and these ideas did not necessarily match their parents' aspirations. In order to achieve a future of independence, individualism, autonomy, and American identity, they believed it necessary to continue learning, whether in high schools or through alternative venues like night school or settlement house classes. When their newly felt responsibility to themselves ran up against their traditional responsibility to their families, many adolescent immigrants faced difficult decisions about which took precedence.

Adolescents at Work. Economic reality and household finances underlay virtually all immigrant adolescents' experiences throughout the period of mass immigration. Although the legal age for work was raised at the beginning of the twentieth century, the practical impact on adolescent workers was minimal. In Lowell, Massachusetts, for instance, after 1901 the mills were subject to a state law that did not allow adolescents between fourteen and eighteen to hold mill jobs unless they could also prove school attendance. But in a town entirely centered on the mill economy, families, school officials, and mill bosses all found it easy to circumvent these rules. Full-time adolescent employment remained common. The legal age of employment in Rhode Island rose from thirteen in 1902 to fourteen in 1907 and to fifteen during the 1920s, which may have encouraged some immigrants to complete a year or two of high school. Still, by 1915 in Providence, 95 percent of Italian boys over fifteen and 78 percent of Italian girls over fifteen were working.

Sixty-seven percent of Jewish boys and 58 percent of Jewish girls over fifteen also worked.[2] With needy families and employers alike opposed to child labor laws—though for very different reasons— enforcement of existing legislation developed very slowly. When the Supreme Court declared that the 1916 Keating-Owen Act, which had indirectly prohibited child labor, was unconstitutional, progressive reformers mourned but few were surprised.

Significant numbers of immigrants at the turn of the century arrived as adolescents on their own and had no choice but to look for work immediately. In 1910 as many as 68,000 adolescents in New York lived in boardinghouses or rented rooms rather than residing with their families.[3] One study reported that 32.1 percent of Mexican migrants were under thirteen years of age when they first crossed the U.S. border. Many of these children likely came with at least one parent or older sibling. But of the 21.8 percent who first came to America between the ages of thirteen and eighteen, a sizable proportion came alone and sought employment immediately.[4] As soon as he arrived, Taro Murato joined a railroad gang of 2,000 young Japanese men, earning $1.25 for nine hours of work a day. He lived in a car on the railroad track and belonged to a group that paid one boy to cook for the rest of them. At age seventeen, Steve Madich joined a group of his friends in Yugoslavia and journeyed all the way to a Pittsburgh mine where one of his friend's brothers worked. They all quickly found jobs loading coal ten hours a day for $3.00.

Due to the popularity of the *padrone* system, especially in Greece and Italy, some adolescent boys arrived with jobs already waiting for them, with employers who had paid their fares. The stereotypical shoeshine boy in New York at the turn of the century arrived through this system. He was met at the docks by the *padrone* and taken to a room shared with several other boys, usually from the same hometown or region. He arose every day by 5:30 a.m. and had only a little time before the shoeshine shop opened at 6.

With only very short breaks for lunch, he worked until 9 or 10 p.m. After the shop closed, he still had to mop the floors, clean the shoeshine stands, and wash and dry the rags. For this grueling work schedule, shoeshine boys earned wages of $110 to $180 a year, out of which they had to pay the *padrone* for meals. The *padrone* tried to restrict their activities, but most of the shoeshine boys managed to learn English and often found better jobs. A similar system was in place for Mexican shoeshine boys in Los Angeles.

Like the shoeshine boys who eventually moved into better jobs and made more money, other immigrants who arrived as adolescents had different economic experiences than those who arrived as adults. They generally assimilated well into the labor market and often ended up succeeding as much as native-born children. Learning skills in the United States rather than abroad presented immigrant children and adolescents with a decided advantage. Joseph Baccardo, for instance, who first came to America in 1898 at age ten, got a job as a barber's apprentice that at first paid only fifty cents a week. As he learned how to cut hair and shave men in the "American style," his wages gradually increased over a period of a few years to six dollars a week. When the boss of his shop died the year Joseph was nineteen, he took over the business himself. At age thirteen, Saul Kaplan immigrated alone in 1890, and on his second day in the United States went to work in a Philadelphia shoe factory. As he learned to read and write English and to operate increasingly complicated machinery, he moved from job to job, each time improving his wages and working conditions. From the shoe factory he went on to a brush factory and then to a button factory. What Saul really wanted was a job in a business where he could learn something. He eventually followed his brother to New York and found a white-collar supervisory job that called on all the skills he had learned as a young immigrant worker.

Immigrant adolescents faced the same dangerous conditions as their adult co-workers. Eighteen Italian parishioners from the Our

At five cents a shine, and with lots of competition, these young shoe blacks in Los Angeles in 1911 were unlikely to earn a steady income. *(Bancroft Library, University of California, Berkeley)*

Lady of Pompei Church in Greenwich Village died in the Triangle Shirtwaist Factory fire in 1911, including several adolescent girls. The 1914 Pittsburgh Survey reported thousands of industrial accidents involving adolescents. Freak (albeit preventable) disasters like the Triangle fire notwithstanding, boys' work was usually more dangerous than girls' work. One fourteen-year-old boy was run over in the steel mill yards and another was caught in a brewery pulley belt. A thirteen-year-old brickyard boy slipped and fell into a tempering machine. Girls were less likely to work around such heavy machinery, with the important exception of textile mills.

Immigrant girls took different kinds of jobs but worked almost as much as immigrant boys. Work opportunities for girls varied but were plentiful. In mill towns like Scranton and Wilkes-Barre, significant numbers of immigrant girls between twelve and sixteen held jobs in 1904 at a time when in the state of Pennsylvania fewer than 10 percent of girls the same age worked.[5]

As a result of gender distinctions in the labor market, in some cases adolescent girls had an even easier time finding jobs than boys. The 1910 Census found that unmarried boys between the ages of fifteen and seventeen were more likely to live at home than girls of the same age because so many adolescent girls lived out at their domestic service jobs.[6] The demand for domestic servants was steady. In 1887 a Danish politician visiting the United States observed:

> The demand for Scandinavian girls, especially Danish ones, is enormous. Mr. Lambke in New York told me that I was welcome to send 3,000 girls any day I pleased. He promised to get them all work within a few days at a beginning wage of seven to twelve dollars [per month].[7]

These were not terrible wages since room and board were included.

Entrepreneurial girls expanded their domestic skills on the job or parlayed them into better kinds of work. Elizabeth Dolan, an Irish nursemaid in Boston, used her weekly free evening to take cooking classes, and Anna Ohlson, a Norwegian girl on the Midwestern prairies, quit her domestic service job to work on a cook car. A threshing crew hired her to travel with them and provide meals. The work was hard since she had to provide meat and potatoes for breakfast, sandwiches, doughnuts, and coffee for the midmorning snack, a big noon meal, another snack, and a large dinner, but she made considerably more money than she could have performing housework.

Not all girls found employment success, of course. The sex trade loomed large as an economic niche for destitute young women. A small number of girls fell prey to forced prostitution. In 1898, Chun Ho testified before the U.S. Commissioner of Immigration about her dark immigration story. At nineteen she and her mother had both been fooled by a procuress's glowing account of life in California. Chun Ho and six other Cantonese girls arrived in San Francisco, where they were taken at first to a seemingly respectable family and then sold to brothels. A Chinese brothel owner bought Chun Ho for nearly two thousand dollars in gold and promised her freedom after four years or a sizable ransom. She did not wait that long before running away to a Christian rescue home. At the time of her testimony, in Chinatown there was still a price on her head.

"White slavery," as it was called, was a real concern, especially for immigrant girls who traveled alone. The safety of family remained central from the perspectives of both government officials and immigrants. When fourteen-year-old Sylvia Bernstein emigrated from Austria in 1914, she planned to join the brother who had preceded her to New York and had sent her ticket money. In order to enter the United States, she had to pass herself off as sixteen so she could immigrate as a woman alone. She also had to allay Ellis Island officials' fears about white slavery by proving that she recognized her brother. Adolescent boys faced fewer obstacles in arriving alone, as immigration officials assumed boys could fend for themselves. Public opinion feared for independent girls working as sewing-machine operators much more than independent boys working as shoe shiners or newsboys.

Adolescents' employment rate continued to rise at the beginning of the twentieth century. In general, girls in America were 72 percent more likely to work in 1910 than in 1872, with more than 50 percent of all African-American girls, 40 percent of all immigrant girls, and just under 20 percent of native-born girls working.[8] Still, other changes affected the labor of all immigrant adolescents. The nature of girls' work shifted within immigrant groups, as did the hours of work for all adolescents. Italian girls gradually moved from unskilled laborers to factory workers, and Jewish girls moved from

jobs in the garment industry to clerical and retail positions. Growing state interest in labor legislation gradually diminished the hours
of labor. When Nathan Cohen immigrated in 1912, all the jobs he
found demanded brutal hours daily. But when his sister Ruth immigrated in 1921, the jobs available to her required nine or ten hours
instead of twelve or fourteen, leaving her time to go to night school.

Regardless of specific working hours, in most households oper-
ating on the principle of the family economy, parental and especially paternal authority remained paramount. Adolescents were
expected to turn over their entire paychecks for the good of the
family. Catherine Balestrieri, who went to work at the Phoenix
Hosiery factory in Milwaukee after finishing eighth grade, gave her
pay envelope to her parents and had to ask her mother for money
when she wanted a soda or ice cream. As one boy explained,

> When you work, you understand, you used to bring your pay
> home and give it to your parents. And whatever they feel they
> want to give you, they decide. There was no disagreement. That
> was their style. And don't you talk about paying board, especially
> in your dad's house. If you want to pay board you have to go
> somewhere else. "This is no boarding house. This is a family," my
> father would say.[9]

Stymied by their attempts to pay board and thereby earn some independence, some adolescents engaged in creative accounting with
their wages. Mollie, a Jewish girl in New York, never told her
mother about her overtime earnings; she kept the money to spend
on herself. Even this mild rebellion was difficult to sustain, however, since she had a hard time explaining where her new feathered
hat came from.

Once children began earning more than their parents, a shift in
family dynamics might have been expected and indeed sometimes
caused problems. But in families that automatically pooled all resources, it mattered less who made the most money and more who

decided how it would be spent. At thirteen, Herschel Roskolenko went to work rather than to high school because, as a trainee riveter during World War I, he could earn three times as much as his father, a coat presser. Herschel and his parents knew that with defense-related wages high during the war, Herschel's work could enable all his other siblings to stay in school. Herschel probably vacillated between resenting the responsibilities that deprived him of his own chance for education and taking pride in the fact that his contributions to the family provided his brothers and sisters with greater opportunity for schooling.

The Elusive Goal of Education. As the Roskolenko family discovered, even the free public schools that America promised immigrants remained out of reach for many adolescents. Not until the 1930s did most high-school-age Americans graduate from high school, and working-class adolescents were far less likely than their middle-class counterparts to complete secondary schooling. In his 1922 book *The Selective Nature of American Secondary Education*, George S. Counts pointed out that immigrant children were the least likely of all to go to high school. He noted that Jewish, Irish, and German adolescents maintained somewhat better records but that Italian, Polish, and Slavic adolescents rarely graduated.[10] Other studies bore out these conclusions. One reported that before World War I, fewer than 2 percent of Slavic adolescents attended high school.[11] The percentage of Italian children in the graduating class at South Philadelphia High School rose from 5 percent in 1918 to 28 percent in 1932, but it should have been much higher given the large Italian population of South Philadelphia.[12] The depression played a role in the much higher 1932 percentage, as more students stayed in high school when jobs were no longer available to them.

Counts also noticed other distinctions within high school populations. He pointed out that among native-born adolescents, girls were more likely to go to high school, but that was not necessarily the case among immigrants. He also demonstrated that immigrant girls were much less likely to do college preparatory work. In some cases, it simply did not occur to immigrant families to continue their older children's education. In more cases, the immediate gain of adolescents' wages far outweighed the potential benefits of extended education. Not even school attendance laws effectively compelled parents to send their children to high school. In Massachusetts in 1906, for example, an estimated 25,000 fourteen- to sixteen-year-olds did not attend school despite compulsory education laws.[13]

Gender limited educational expectations and opportunities for immigrant youth. Both boys and girls were potential producers of income, but because boys had access to the more lucrative male labor market, they were generally less likely to stay in school. Korean siblings Mary and Meung Paik together were the first to graduate from the elementary school in their mining town, but only Mary had the opportunity to continue her formal education. Their father felt bad about requiring his son Meung's help to support the family, but he had no choice. As a boy, Meung could find work on road crews that was not available to Mary, who left home to attend high school feeling guilty that no work she could do would effectively help her family. But gender conventions could also restrict girls' education. Clara Corica recalled that in Cleveland's Little Italy, girls were forbidden to go to English or citizenship classes because of the lack of suitable chaperonage. Elvira Adorno went to high school in Brooklyn but was allowed to take only the classes her father approved as appropriate for her.

Different immigrant groups had different ideas about their children's educational opportunities. Italian and Mexican girls sometimes went to work within their communities because their parents were so concerned about the absence of proper chaperonage at school or in more public workplaces. Their brothers might end up with greater educational opportunity as a result of their sisters' contributions to the family income. A young writer to the *Jewish Daily Forward*'s advice column begged for help in recovering from the guilt he felt over the tragic death of his older sister in the Triangle Shirtwaist Factory fire. Their parents had decided that she should go to work so that her younger brother could stay in school, since with an education he would have more career options than any girl could have. The editor advised that the boy should certainly continue his education in honor of his sister's sacrifice.

Family needs and expectations were such a critical factor in access to education that one historian has argued that immigrant children and adolescents who lived in orphanages or other nonfamilial settings actually had a better chance to obtain an education. That was Bessie Jeong's experience. Her older sister was pressured into an arranged marriage, but when fourteen-year-old Bessie left home in 1915 and fled to the Presbyterian Mission Home in San Francisco, she found support for not only her high school education but also her college and medical school aspirations. Private institutions like the Presbyterian Mission Home attracted adolescent students by combining educational opportunity with other well-established sets of values. By the mid-1890s, Detroit's Felician Academy provided secondary education to Polish girls who wished to become Felician sisters. A parallel boys' school offered secondary education to aspiring priests. These were the only secondary schools in Michigan to teach in Polish, satisfying parents who could rest assured that their children would graduate with fluency in both their native tongue and their religion, with job security in that most important of ethnic institutions, the church.

Despite all the factors working against them, a great many immigrant adolescents did attend high school. By one count the urban high school population increased 711 percent from 1890 to 1918, and in many places the majority of students had foreign-born fathers.[14] Recalling his high school days at Central High in Cleveland, the Harlem Renaissance poet Langston Hughes noted that virtually all his classmates were immigrants whose ethnic and religious differences often prompted conflict. He thought the only reason he won the class elections for president was because as an African American he was a compromise candidate, seen as neither Christian nor Jew. In New York, Leonard Covello's 1907 Morris High School graduation class included students from a wide variety of ethnic backgrounds. For every classmate like Hilda M. Von Hartmann, Charles O'Neil, Gertrude Baumgart, or Frank Saporito, there were undoubtedly dozens of others who never made it to high school at all. Still, though immigrant adolescents who attended high school had to overcome economic and sometimes familial obstacles to get there, once they arrived they became eager students. In San Francisco, Japanese boys and girls scored higher than native-born American children in their knowledge of American history and literature.

Some immigrant parents supported their children's educational achievements no matter where they might lead. A Polish farm wife in Michigan who barely spoke English herself had sixteen children who never went to school, but of one daughter she said, "When I marry I swear I make one girl school-teacher in this country." The whole family pooled its meager resources to support that daughter through high school.[15] Everyone understood that education could pave the way to a better life, or at least to better employment options. Japanese and Korean boys attending Honolulu's McKinley High School in 1922 overwhelmingly hoped their education would help them become professionals or at least skilled workers rather than farmers and laborers. In rural areas, however, the better life to which education might lead could often only be found elsewhere. Between 1921 and 1926, thirty-two of the forty-four high school graduates in a rural Danish community in Minnesota left the community to seek opportunities in an urban area.[16]

As much as adolescents longed for more education, either with or without family support, they understood that extended schooling might widen the gap between them and their parents. An edu-

cator himself as an adult, Leonard Covello worked tirelessly to in-
corporate Italian into the curricular offerings because he remembered how alienated he felt from his own family and ethnic heritage
when he had to take German in high school. Immigrant pastor
Constantine Panunzio failed in his attempt to convince Italian boys
and girls to leave their homes and attend special secondary schools
because parents and children alike feared the consequences of such
rigid separation from Italian family life and culture. For some immigrants, education did not hold enough intrinsic value to make it
worth the sacrifice.

While Panunzio's initiative failed, other educational programs
achieved more success in broadening access to high school education for immigrant adolescents. In the 1920s the Chaffey Union
High School in California set up a traveling schoolroom on a bus.
With the seats removed, fitted out with folding chairs and a black-
board, the high school on wheels traveled to migrant farm camps,
summoning teenage students with a reverberating gong. From 1903
to 1910 even the federal government became involved in expanding
the population of high school students, bringing Filipino boys to
the United States for education and practical training. Many of
these *pensionados*, as they were known, had attended American elementary schools in the Philippines. Salvadore del Fierro recalled,
"From the time of kindergarten on our islands . . . we stood in our
short pants and saluted the Stars and Stripes which waved over our
schoolyards."[17] Coming to the United States to continue their education became a desirable goal for young would-be immigrants.

As was the case for their younger siblings, immigrant adolescents combined work and education if that was the only way to stay
in school. When Ernesto Galarza's mother died and he went to live
with a relative, he was expected both to contribute to the household
and to earn his high school diploma. Since he was the oldest boy,
his family was determined that Ernesto would graduate. Education
always took precedence over work, but he nonetheless had to pay

for his own schoolbooks and clothing. During his high school years in Sacramento, Ernesto took a variety of jobs. He carried water, chopped wood, cleaned houses, stacked boxes, and delivered drugstore supplies. No matter what his current job, he kept his eye on his real goal: going to college.

Mary Paik could not have attended high school without working her way through, either. She had to leave her family's mining town for a town sixty miles away that had the closest high school. Mary looked for a job that would provide room and board if she worked after school and on weekends for no other pay. She awoke every day at 5 a.m. to make breakfast and lunch for the man of the house and then cleaned the house and cooked for the other family members. Until she could scrape together enough money, Mary could not afford schoolbooks; she spent her lunch hours copying the next day's material from a classmate's texts. After her first year, Mary's father refused to let her return to such difficult circumstances. She continued high school elsewhere, working all the while.

For most immigrant adolescents, work took precedence over secondary education. They turned to alternative forms of education to continue their schooling. Night school became a common means of learning English for immigrants who arrived as adolescents and had to go straight to work. Demetrius Paleologas left Greece in 1915, traveling to St. Louis to work in his father's friend's restaurant. He depended on night school to learn English since everyone in the restaurant spoke Greek. Sadie Frowne, thirteen when she first came to the United States from Poland, left her first job as a domestic servant to take a factory job that would free up her evenings to learn English at night school. As was the case in regular high schools, certain immigrant groups were more likely to take advantage of night school classes. In 1906, Jews constituted a majority of the 100,000 students in New York City's night schools, and a 1912 study estimated that 95 percent of Pittsburgh's night

Working girls of all nationalities make the best of their spare evening hours in this crowded night school classroom in Boston, 1909. *(Library of Congress)*

school students were Jewish. Women made up about 40 percent of night school students overall.[18]

Regardless of their ethnic or national background, most night school students made learning English their first priority. As John Foster Carr's *Guide to the United States for the Jewish Immigrant* cautioned, "you cannot be in America a single day without understanding the necessity of speaking the same language that all other men in America speak."[19] Night school provided other learning opportunities too. Hull House and other settlement houses offered night classes in both academic and vocational subjects specifically for adolescents. At Hull House, Hilda Satt learned how to compose essays and how to dance. Large philanthropic institutions like the Educational Alliance in New York were veritable temples of alternative education through evening classes. From the 1890s on, the Alliance's largest enrollments came in practical classes like English, typing, stenography, business arithmetic, and cooking, but interested students could also take courses in science, art, history, and literature. A large reading room and library were available as well as a roof garden for parties. The department of physical education ran separate swimming pools for men and women and offered classes in calisthenics and weight training. Discussion groups considered every conceivable topic, from Zionism to the techniques of poultry farming.

The most ambitious—and luckiest—immigrant adolescents used night school as a stepping-stone to more conventional forms of education. John Daroubian, a fifteen-year-old refugee from Armenia, went to night school in New York as soon as he arrived in 1919 but then went to high school and eventually to Columbia University. Maurice Hindus, frustrated by his failure to teach himself English with a Russian-English dictionary, stuck it out in night school even though he and many of his fellow students had trouble staying awake after a long day's work. As soon as Maurice felt able, he took his newly acquired language skills to Stuyvesant High School for a regular secondary education.

Like other immigrant students in their high schools and colleges, John and Maurice were able to graduate only through a combination of hard work, perseverance, family support, and good luck. Their ability to move from a combination of work and night classes to full-time high school or college illustrates the constantly shifting parameters of adolescents' responsibilities. Immigrant families tried to take advantage of as many opportunities as possible. When economic circumstances allowed, parents released their adolescent children from their family economic responsibilities and permitted, even encouraged, them to attend to their own personal development. This fluidity helped preserve immigrant families even as adolescents negotiated the conflicting expectations of their home, work, school, and peer environments.

The Battle over Identity

From the perspective of the fervent advocates of the Americanization movement in the early twentieth century, immigrants living in the United States had a responsibility to forsake all vestiges of the Old World and immerse themselves in the New. Giving up on immigrant adults as hopelessly old-fashioned, agents of Americanization concentrated instead on immigrant youth, using their desire for success as a platform to encourage radical assimilation. Immigrants who could not be absorbed into the body politic or social, such as Asian or Mexican immigrants perceived as racially distinct, received less attention but were nonetheless expected to conform to basic social and cultural standards of Americanization. Adolescents encountered repeated messages that the only way for them to succeed was to turn their backs on their ethnic past and embrace a homogenized American future.

Immigrant communities of course resisted such entreaties. In addition to the emphasis on language schools and holiday celebrations that helped keep younger children attached to their ethnic backgrounds, communities showed their concern for adolescents by highlighting religious and ethnic coming-of-age rituals that would bind them to tradition as they moved toward adulthood. Overall, however, these efforts met with little success. Adolescents may not have set out to rid themselves of all their ethnic affiliations, and most probably would have denied such a desire. Yet the call of Americanization was strong, and most immigrant adolescents succumbed one way or another. Since their parents, too, wished to succeed in their new home, they found it difficult to set boundaries that would provide their children with greater guidance about how to balance identities.

The generation gap that almost inevitably arose from such circumstances was a source of great pain for immigrant parents and adolescents alike. Immigration alone did not create this tension; turn-of-the-century American households of all kinds faced changing family dynamics as a consequence of the growing recognition of adolescence as a distinct stage of life between childhood and adulthood. But the immigrant experience did complicate the issues. The conflicts that arose were so intense that in some cases state intervention was necessary to try to resolve them.

Adolescents and Acculturation. Americanization confronted immigrant children at very early ages, but in some ways it posed the greatest challenges to adolescents. If they immigrated as adolescents, particularly if they came without parents or alone, they sometimes found that they literally could not survive unless they acculturated rapidly. Many were happy to do so. As one Jewish girl wrote in 1916,

> The longer I live in America the more I think of the question of Americanising the immigrant. At first I thought that there is not such a question as that, for the children of immigrants naturally are Americans and good Americans. America is a land made up of foreigners and the virtues of American life is the best Americaniser.

For this girl and countless others like her, "America means for an Immigrant a fairy promised land that came out true."[20] There was no reason to resist the push to Americanize when the pull was so strong.

The push came from many sources. Civic, industrial, educational, and political leaders all agreed that the desirable outcome for immigrants was assimilation. The prominent businessman Chauncey Depew, president of the New York Central and Hudson

River Railroad, explained in an 1888 speech that the goals for immigrant children were clear: "Let the boys be the trained soldiers of constitutional freedom, the girls the intelligent mothers of freemen, and the sons of the anarchists will become the bulwarks of the law."[21] The only way to protect against foreign ideas was to transform the foreigners, or at least their children, into firm believers in traditional American values of liberty, family, and democracy.

Religious leaders worked to add Christian godliness to the mix. A set of 1921 photographs from the Pennsylvania church mission in an immigrant community underlines this point. The first photo shows "The Raw Material," a group of Italian children and adolescents dressed in rags, looking unkempt, unschooled, and unpromising. The second photo, labeled "Two Years Later," shows the same children, smiling, better groomed, and dressed in proper American clothing. The caption points out "what Church influence can do in the way of American refinement." Religion was important both for its own sake and as a means of moving immigrant children into godly American lives.[22] A commentator on the "Second-Generation Dilemmas" of Chinese Americans noted that the most successful immigrant children and adolescents were usually those whose families benefited from early contact with Christian missionaries who helped them learn English and American customs quickly.

The vast majority of Americans agreed strongly with the sentiment that immigrants, if they must come at all, owed their new home not only their allegiance but also their rapid acculturation. The Civic Club of Philadelphia spoke for many when it reported in 1910, with deep satisfaction, that it was becoming difficult even to analyze the needs of local Scandinavian immigrants: their children were so Americanized they could not be distinguished from any other children. From within the Scandinavian families, though, things may not have been so simple. Ruth Dahl remembered being "cut off from my parents' world in Sweden and Norway and from the things that happened to my family before I was old enough to experience them myself." The Dahls' family dynamics were irretrievably disrupted by the children's process of Americanization. Mother Emma Dahl raised six children on her own, yet she still deferred to her Americanized older daughters Olive and Elsie for any big decisions. It was Elsie, for instance, who decided in 1915 that her younger sister Ruth would go to college.[23] This disruption of parental authority actually met with approval from agents of Americanization, who had given up on immigrant parents but assumed that immigrant children would conform in order to succeed.

Critics of the Americanization movement in the period of mass immigration point to the high degree of social control on immigrant families exerted by the agents and institutions of assimilation. No doubt the pressure to become American was powerful and had a major impact on immigrant youth. Insistence on a particular type of Americanization—essentially acculturation into middle-class social and cultural norms—was so important to native-born Americans because it reinforced the superiority of their own life patterns. The content of commonly used textbooks in night school classes confirmed the ideological bent of instruction in English designed to head directly toward middle-class family values. The 1909 text *English for Foreigners* consisted of a series of simple sentences that imparted such wisdom. One lesson read:

> This is the family in the sitting room. The family is made up of the father, the mother, and the children. That is the father who is reading. The father is the husband. That is the mother who is sewing. The mother is the wife. The father and mother are the parents. The sister is playing the piano. The brother is standing beside her. The family makes the home.[24]

The class and gender implications of these language lessons were important components of the education offered to immigrants by the night schools.

Children and adolescents were natural targets for such Americanization efforts, as it was assumed they could influence their families and home life. Girls and boys exerted different kinds of influences, however, since the expectation was that they would be primarily responsible for private and public domains, respectively. For instance, a baby-care class for tenth-grade immigrant girls in Utah aimed not only to teach them to sew layette items but also to encourage them to persuade their mothers to abandon traditional swaddling clothes for modern baby outfits. Pointing to the mixture of ethnic groups represented at any given urban school, educators used classrooms as incubators of American social and cultural norms. At one Lower East Side school, a journalist noted in 1903 that "The different races are so scattered" that the differences among the students faded in comparison to the American interests they inevitably held in common, such as the boys' "intense common interest in party and city politics."[25] The journalist approved, hoping the boys would eventually parlay these political interests into participation in public life.

It would be a mistake to think that all movement toward Americanization and acculturation was forced upon immigrant youth or even their families and communities. Immigrants reacted with ambivalence to the rampant pressure to Americanize. Even within ethnic groups, debate raged over the best approach to living in a new land. Among Greek immigrants, for example, the American Hellenic Educational Progressive Association advocated acculturation and urged widespread nationalization while the Greek American Progressive Association supported Greek language schools and the maintenance of Greek customs in the home. In practice, most Greek families adopted a middle road, but joining one or the other of the ethnic associations did make a statement. Adolescents too expressed ambivalence. Mar Sui Haw, a Chinese boy living in Seattle, laughed in 1924 that "Chinese women who are born here are regular flappers," and he professed to be thoroughly Americanized himself. Still, he hastened to add, he wanted to marry a traditional Chinese girl.[26]

Whatever the consequences, some degree of integration seemed desirable to most immigrant families. Americanization took a variety of forms, both external and internal. For Mexicans in the Southwest, acculturation became obvious when young people married and set up new households containing such "American" items as iron stoves and record players. Clothing also served as an indicator of Americanization. One of the Pittsburgh Survey authors noted that in the Russian community, girls adopted American clothes and hairstyles as soon as they arrived in the United States. Immigrant girls working in garment factories in New York gained early knowledge about the latest styles; they tried to reproduce them as inexpensively as possible. In the photos that immigrants took of their families, the children usually wore American clothes, though they might also wear jewelry or symbols with connections to their homelands. Formal portraits of Norwegian adolescent girls and women, for instance, typically showed them wearing a *sølje*, a traditional silver brooch, on their starched American shirtwaists.

Names also indicated Americanization. If parents bestowed ethnic names, their adolescent children changed them to suit their own purposes, as in shortening Makato to Mac or translating Yuriko as Lily. Growing up in Berkeley, Yoshiko Uchida wished desperately for a "name like Mary Anne Brown or Betty Johnson."[27] Marcus Ravage, a Jewish boy who came to the United States in 1900 at age sixteen, believed that "The first step toward Americanization was to fall into one or the other of the two great tribes of Rosies and Annies." Food was another indicator of acculturation. Marcus could hardly believe his eyes when he found that the relatives with whom he boarded really did eat meat every day, along with unfamiliar new American foods like bananas and cauliflower.[28] Since ethnic foods were among the few contributions to American culture that even the oldest-stock Americans were willing to admit, cross-ethnic food mixing became a further sign of acculturation.

Immigrant communities understood their children's acculturation not just as a potential threat to tradition but also as a valuable contribution to the success of their ethnic communities in America. When the Polish Youth Alliance of America was founded in 1894, it included among its goals preserving Polish culture, setting up Polish reading rooms, supporting Polish singing groups, and celebrating Polish national holidays. But the community also hoped the young Pole in America would

> honor and admire this land which nourishes and feeds him, let him sing the praises of this land whose bread he eats. . . . Let him become acclimated, let him adapt himself to new forms of dress, amusements and customs—in a word, let him create a new and distinct type of American Pole![29]

Many other ethnic groups agreed with this approach, taking special care to point out what a contribution their children could make to their new country. As a Ukrainian writer put it, "Ukrainian youth in the United States is already an entirely different kind of Ukrainian youth. But from this type of youth, America prospers and grows."[30]

Immigrant parents remained concerned about maintaining their own cultures and encouraging American appreciation for ethnic heritage and tradition. The Czech-American Central School Association declared its purpose to "educate our adolescents so that they associate with Americans, and spread information among them regarding the Czech nation and its national aims."[31] This goal too could not be accomplished in a completely insular ethnic community. With very few exceptions, immigrant adolescents did not lead lives apart from American society or culture, nor did they or their families wish to do so. Immigrants were acutely aware that their native-born children were citizens of the United States. The first editorial of the Japanese-American *Hawaii Hochi* in 1912 announced:

> It will be one of the principal aims of this paper, to afford an opportunity to such young people to learn all of the important affairs of the United States, and become familiar with its institutions, so that they may not only enjoy the privileges of citizenship to the fullest extent, but may become patriotic citizens, of intelligence, integrity, and virtue.[32]

Japanese parents may have felt the prerogatives of their children's citizenship most keenly, since they were denied the possibility of becoming citizens themselves. Still, it was for these privileges that many immigrants came to the United States in the first place.

The issue of citizenship provided a clear example of the ways in which race and gender identity shaped the meaning of Americanization for immigrant adolescents. Unless born in the United States, Asian adolescents could not become citizens throughout the period of mass immigration. Before the Nineteenth Amendment granted women suffrage in 1920, citizenship was limited for girls and women, who could not vote. Until the Cable Act of 1922, American-born daughters of immigrants found their citizenship status threatened if they married noncitizens. Even after the Cable Act, marriage to Asian-born men ineligible for naturalization would also lead to a revocation of women's citizenship. Americanization for immigrant girls presented them with the same obstacles to full legal and political citizenship status as their native-born female counterparts. No matter what proponents of Americanization might have said, the process of reshaping official and personal identity was far from simple.

Religious Coming-of-Age Rituals. The deep religious roots of most immigrant communities provided a further complication for adolescents who were considering the advantages of jettisoning their immigrant backgrounds. Freedom of religion was one of many motivations for immigrating in the first place, so immigrant parents liked to point out to their children that practicing their religious heritage in traditional ways should not retard their process of acculturation. Ethnic communities strengthened traditional loyalties by making special celebrations or religious ceremonies the most persistent social rituals for adolescents. Twelfth birthdays in Japanese culture, twelfth (for girls) or thirteenth (for boys) birthdays in Jewish culture, and tenth and fifteenth birthdays in Chinese culture were all coming-of-age markers. Various ethnic Protestant and Catholic churches elevated confirmation to a new level of importance in an effort to associate adolescence with tradition as well as autonomy. The form of the celebrations or ceremonies sometimes combined Old and New World traditions in ways similar to other forms of cultural blending common among immigrants. Parents were no less susceptible to syncretization than their children and did not, in any case, reject all aspects of American life.

The development of the bat mitzvah for Jewish girls provides one case study of these dynamics at work. Ancient Jewish sources specified that girls reached the age of legal and religious responsibility at twelve and boys at thirteen. For centuries, boys across the global Jewish diaspora had marked their bar mitzvahs as thirteen-year-olds, typically performing some set of public religious functions reserved for males deemed adult by Jewish law. But twelve-year-old girls, though equally responsible as adults according to Jewish law, historically did not commemorate their coming of age with parallel rituals. Not until 1922 did the first bat mitzvah ceremony take place in the United States, and it was such a departure from tradition that it became popular only gradually.

Those Jewish families that did choose bat mitzvah ceremonies for their daughters were clearly influenced by the coeducational environment of the United States. They were also affected by the nineteenth-century development of confirmation ceremonies for

adolescents adopted by Reform Judaism, which in turn were modeled on ceremonies conducted by many Protestant denominations
in America. As one confirmand remembered the Christian ritual:

> One of the events in the lives of the Germans from Russia and in
> the life of the church was the ceremony of Confirmation. . . .
> Youngsters after they became fourteen or fifteen years of age went
> to the Confirmation class, which the minister conducted, and boy
> am I telling you, you had to learn years of Confirmation catechism
> that you had to study. . . . On Palm Sunday you had to march in to
> the front of the church, sit down and when the appropriate time
> came, the minister quizzed each one of us. . . . On Easter Sunday
> we would dress up in our new suits, the girls in their nice new
> white dresses with flowers, and . . . we were allowed to take Com-
> munion for the first time.[33]

Public religious ceremonies like bar and bat mitzvahs and confirma-
tions not only served religious purposes; they also socialized adolescents into religious and ethnic groups at a time in their lives when
parents were most afraid of them abandoning their communities.

Parents feared that the lure of America's secular society would
win over their children's souls. Their fears were well grounded. Flora
Belle Jan of Fresno broke her traditional Chinese mother's heart
when, after accompanying her to visit the shrine of an ancestor, she
"decided it was time to stop this foolish custom. So I got up and
slammed down the rice in front of the idol and said, 'So long Old
Top, I don't believe in you anymore.' "[34] Immigrant parents found
that their children's attraction to American life and culture threatened religious continuity. Investing their coming of age with religious meaning was an attempt to close the gap between parents and
children, but the results were mixed at best.

The Generation Gap. The lack of sympathy between parents and
children in immigrant families was of great concern to communal

workers. While promoting children's rights and obligations to learn as a means of family acculturation, they also acknowledged the deleterious effects of teaching children to look down on traditional customs and values. A 1916 article in the *S.E.G. News*, a publication for Italian and Jewish girls, cautioned that "a girl should never be ashamed of her home or surroundings."[35] The social and cultural ideals that immigrant children learned at school and in Americanizing community institutions created family rifts between expectations and needs, ideals and realities. Solutions to the generation gap only rarely presented themselves. One Philadelphia school did its best by celebrating the life and customs of Italy as well as America in order to encourage their mostly Italian students' pride in both old and new countries. For many immigrant families, however, the rift between parents and children was not so easily minimized. As immigrant children came of age, they fought to make their own choices as individuals rather than as members of family units, an indication of the impact of the American ethos of individualism on their lives.

For adolescents who immigrated by themselves, the mere act of leaving the old country opened a geographical gap that might never be crossed. Julia Goniprow recalled that when she left Lithuania in 1891 as a teenager, "My mother came with me to the railroad station. When we said good-bye, she said it was just like seeing me go into my casket. I never saw her again."[36] Young Japanese immigrant Choki Oshiro had a different experience when he left Okinawa. His mother took him to the Emigration Agency and sang and danced as his ship embarked. She believed he was heading toward a better life. Still, the end result was the same. Choki never saw his mother again, either.

The chasm of the oceans loomed wide for adolescents who immigrated alone, but those who came with their families also faced the differences imposed by language differences. Few children found themselves literally unable to speak to their parents. They

were much more likely to serve as interpreters in every sense of the
word. Even young immigrant children translated for their parents,
who were almost always slower to learn English, but early adolescents were the most likely of all to take on a nearly official role
as interpreter. A study of truancy in Chicago found that many
twelve-, thirteen-, and fourteen-year-olds missed school because
they were at home accompanying their mothers to court or helping
their fathers rent an apartment. Their parents could not function in
society without their children, who often switched so smoothly
from English to their native language that they had to stop and
think about it before identifying which language they were speaking
at a given moment. Parents' need for their children's knowledge resulted in what Jane Addams, not unsympathetically, referred to as
an "almost pathetic dependence of the family on the child."[37] Other
social commentators were less circumspect in expressing their opinion that when adolescents in particular acted as interpreters for
their parents, they were "thrown into a position of unnatural importance" that destroyed traditional family dynamics.[38]

Adolescents engaged in cultural as well as literal interpretation.
Under pressure to Americanize, and often ashamed of their backgrounds as a result, they tried to teach their parents how to live as
Americans. Mixed motives of embarrassment and sincere concern
led to scenes such as the one that ensued when a noted Czech vio-
linist performed at Bohemian Hall in New York. As he began to
play the Czech national anthem, children throughout the audience
remonstrated with their parents for displaying too much emotion.
In an agony of embarrassment, they begged their parents to applaud
politely like a respectable American audience. Mothers and daughters suffered similar cultural gaps when shopping together. Adolescent girls found that shopping with mothers who were used to
haggling over prices resulted in mortifying encounters unless they
could explain the concept of fixed prices in department stores.

Social life presented another major source of conflict between the generations. Adolescents rebelled against parents they viewed as unreasonably restrictive in this new land of freedom, while parents did everything they could to keep their children, especially daughters, within a controlled social environment. Sixteen-year-old Henrietta was infuriated when her traditional Mexican father watched over her carefully and would allow only her Mexican girl friends to visit. At eighteen, Jennie Hyatt constantly fought off her mother's attempts to bring in a traditional Jewish matchmaker and partially succeeded only because her brother supported her. Children resisted their parents' efforts to maintain social and cultural traditions, accusing their mothers and fathers of living in the past and warding off change. Yet parents believed they had made the biggest change of all in immigrating to improve their children's lives, only to lose them following their arrival.

Adolescent children could be the despair of immigrant parents. New York parish priest Antonio Demo spent much of each day advising Italian parents who wanted his help controlling their wild "American" children. Boys and girls rebelled against expectations that they would conform to strictures they deemed irrelevant to their lives in America. In Chicago one Mexican girl daily raised the hem of her skirt when she went to school and lowered it before she came home. A social worker had to intervene in the case of an Italian girl who left home because her father would not let her use the gaslight to entertain her friends or read, even though she paid for it. The girl returned home only after the social worker convinced the father that the daughter should be allowed to see friends or read at home after work. In this case a compromise was effected: the girl could do what she wanted as long as she did it within the safe confines of home.

Parents, too, sometimes took steps that exacerbated the generation gap. The historian Robert Orsi has shown that Italian parents sometimes used their heritage as an "instrument of discipline" to demonstrate to children how unsatisfying they were in comparison to children in Italy, where family relations (theoretically) existed in perfect order, with authority and ultimate knowledge invested in the parents. Orsi suggests that at public events like weddings or funerals, where more than one generation gathered, immigrant parents told stories of the old country explicitly to cast aspersions on their children's comfort and high expectations in America.[39] Such an interpretation of the power flow in immigrant families softens the embarrassment and rejection of immigrant children without discounting the very real differences that usually peaked when sons and daughters reached adolescence.

Immigrant adolescents might sympathize with their parents' sacrifices and values. During the early 1920s a visitor found that a group of Bohemian boys in Wisconsin felt guilty for not wanting to be farmers when their parents had worked so hard to make the land viable. Yet they were unwilling to forgo the better future they believed beckoned them through college education, just to live their parents' lives all over again. Sympathy and understanding did not solve the problem of differing expectations and dreams.

When adolescents made every effort to avoid the generation gap by obeying their parents without question, the results were not necessarily salutary for everyone involved. Jane Addams wrote of the "touching fidelity to immigrant parents" that she saw in "a young man who day after day attends ceremonies which no longer express his religious convictions and who makes his vain effort to interest his Russian Jewish father in social problems." Another girl left her job as a stenographer because her parents objected to her working on Saturday, with the result of poverty for all. The parents believed the sacrifice was necessary, but the daughter, though obedient, was less sure.[40] In these two cases, family closeness took precedence because of decisions the children made. But parents had little power to compel such choices, and the consequences when adolescents made different kinds of decisions could be so severe that outside authorities intervened. The removal, even if temporary, of family authority to the state indicated the level of the crisis that Americanization brought to immigrant families.

In this regard the settlement houses and juvenile courts that developed during the Progressive Era were especially active. Before the mass immigration of the late nineteenth century began, an important Illinois Supreme Court decision in 1870 ruled that due process was guaranteed for minors, emphasizing parental rights and undercutting nascent state paternalism by enhancing the rights of children. In the Progressive Era, though, reformers interested in a legal basis for juvenile reform later worked for narrower protections for "social citizenship" benefits such as food, housing, clothing, schooling, and heath care, applying American middle-class standards to all these benefits at the expense of parental rights rooted in immigrant culture. Immigrants took an active role in the way subsequent legal encounters played out in the courts. In one extreme case, a boy from an Italian family appealed to the court to support his opposition to his father's discipline by arguing that as an American-born citizen he should not be subject to beatings by a foreigner (his father).

In many cases, American standards not only of law but of family composition and rights left immigrant families with little recourse. For example, after the father of a Syrian family died in 1910, his relatives accused the mother of abusing her thirteen-year-old daughter. The paternal relatives claimed they should have custody of the girl since according to Syrian tradition the paternal grandfather held the rights to the children. The Massachusetts court that heard the case disagreed, citing the maternal bond as the most important claim, and awarded custody to the mother.

As in the case of the Syrian family, gender often contributed to the shape of immigrants' interaction with the state. Following a series of precedents set at the end of the 1800s, women typically were awarded custody of their children on the assumption that mothers would be better caretakers. Unfortunately for the Syrian girl involved in this case, the court's decision placed her in such physical jeopardy from her abusive mother that she was later removed to custodial care by the Massachusetts Society for Prevention of Cruelty to Children. Even in less extreme situations, gender shaped the very foundation of juvenile and family law. Boys were committed to reformatories until they were eighteen; girls were usually committed only until they turned sixteen. In the Boston Juvenile Court, girls' cases were handled primarily by women supervisors. Girls never appeared alone before a judge and were kept away from the courtroom as much as possible. During its early years the court had no female probation officers and relied instead on female volunteers from the National Council of Jewish Women, the St. Vincent de Paul Society, and the Boston Italian Immigrant Society.

The offenses most often associated with immigrant children and adolescents were also distinguished by gender. Jane Addams noted that in Chicago it was almost always boys who broke into grain freighters, picked coal off the railroad tracks, and burglarized department stores during the Christmas season. She speculated that since boys of all ethnic backgrounds were exposed early and often to an ethic of male providership, they felt responsible for making sure their families had food, fuel, and even fripperies.[41] Commentators on the Polish experience in America pointed out that since children no longer spent all their time within their families and communities, there was little common ground between parents and children in the New World. If anything, they warned, boys' experiences at school, work, and in the street encouraged them to hold their parents in the lowest regard, resulting in family breakdowns that led directly to delinquency. Repeat runaway brothers Joe and John Kansparek of Chicago, who first left home when they were ten and eight years old respectively, led such unhappy home lives that they stole potatoes from the railroad to feed their siblings and then broke into a dry goods store to get clothing. Their father and stepmother

A street-gang corner in Springfield, Massachusetts, 1916. Note the "tough guy" stance of some gang members. *(Library of Congress)*

refused to accept the rulings of their local truant officer or the juvenile court because they insisted that as parents only they should decide how to deal with their children. As adolescents, both brothers eventually ended up living temporarily on the street with a gang of other Polish boys whose families had collapsed under the strain of adapting to a new country and culture.

Adolescent girls stole too, but social workers and court officials were much more concerned about their sexual deviancy. They feared that stricter parental control would lead to sexual rebelliousness, given the "innumerable suggestions of sexual life pervading the city atmosphere." Marien Stepanek, who ran away at age sixteen, eventually returned home but refused to give up her habit of frequenting theaters and movie houses, much to the dismay of both her parents and her social worker, all of whom assumed that Marien's interest in the "high life" indicated that her morality had already been hopelessly compromised. One analysis of such situations concluded that "illicit sexual tendencies are simply a component . . . of a powerful desire for new experience and for general excitement," but this insight was applied only to girls, dismissing boys' experimentation as less destructive or even noteworthy.[42] Fear of girls' sexual deviancy was so great that immigrant families at times turned over their own daughters to the juvenile courts, hoping that the state would supply the supervision or even custodial care they had failed to provide. This disruption of traditional family formation represented one of the most extreme manifestations of the clash between immigrant parents and adolescent children.

The Development of Ethnic Youth Cultures

Another disruption in family formations resulted from immigrant parents' inability to protect their children from discrimination. Reformers could not force native-born Americans to accept even the most Americanized immigrants. Adolescents found prejudice particularly painful because discrimination seemed to them a betrayal of the American promise that if they conformed, they would succeed. That their schoolmates or co-workers would continue to judge them by their national, racial, or ethnic characteristics rather than by their activities, aspirations, and accomplishments taught young immigrants that there were limits to their success as individuals.

Although some adolescents coped with rejection by retreating into their families and communities, they did so on their own Americanized terms. Their strategies included turning inward and creating a vibrant ethnic social life. They combined the emerging American youth culture of the turn of the century, which relied heavily on peers rather than family members, with elements of traditional culture to fashion a modern, ethnic social network of like-minded individuals from similar backgrounds. It was not that adolescent immigrants of one group never interacted with friends from another. Rather, they formed interest groups of peers that ebbed and flowed away from one another based on custom, social needs, loyalty to family and community, and involvement in consumer culture. They asserted their American identity but within the context of their immigrant heritage.

In no other area of social interaction was this more true than the ways in which young immigrants developed courtship, dating, and marriage patterns. Whether foreign-born themselves or the native-born children of immigrants, immigrant adolescents managed to practice new ideas about romantic dating and modern marriage while still choosing partners from similar backgrounds. In preparing to start families of their own, they strove to achieve a balance between the best of the Old World and the New.

Resisting Prejudice. Although immigrant adolescents and their families and communities viewed Americanization as a mostly desirable goal, they rarely met the welcoming reception they sought. American-born immigrant children might have been U.S. citizens by birth, but their legal status offered no guarantee of social acceptance. Some first- and second-generation immigrants encountered discrimination for the first time as adolescents. High school was a turning point in identity for many of them, especially Asians and Mexicans whose perceived racial difference led to social segregation. Since high schools were still the provinces of the privileged during the late 1800s and early 1900s, they typically brought together students from a number of feeder schools, backgrounds, and neighborhoods. For Japanese, Chinese, and Korean adolescents who had spent their childhoods in relatively sheltered communities, discrimination came as a rude awakening both inside and outside school.

Lillie Leung grew up in a mixed neighborhood in San Francisco rather than in Chinatown, one where "she mingled with all the children quite freely, but when I was about twelve years old they began to turn away from me. . . . Up to that time, I never realized that I was any different, but then I began to think about it."[43] A series of early-twentieth-century court decisions had gradually forced public schools to integrate the diverse populations of California, but no court decision could change public opinion, which generally favored keeping Asian and Mexican children in separate schools.

This segregationist climate sometimes divided along generational lines. Unlike Lillie Leung, John Aiso remained sufficiently popular with his adolescent schoolmates that he was elected president of the student body at Le Conte Junior High School in Hollywood. Other students' parents protested so loudly, however, that the principal suspended student government for the year. Aiso went on to be a successful debater at Hollywood High School, but the administration there did not allow him to represent the school at the national finals despite widespread student-body support. Even the acceptance of his peers could not protect Aiso from the discrimination he faced as an adolescent. Another girl recalled that even though she thought she was a popular member of her public school class, none of her schoolmates protested when she was denied entrance to a local beach because she was a "Jap."

Adolescent immigrants faced other forms of outright prejudice. At age thirteen, Pardee Lowe tried to find a summer office job, but he discovered that no one in San Francisco would hire a Chinese boy outside of Chinatown, where office jobs were scarce. Fourteen-year-old Mary Paik, who grew up in Western mining towns, saw her first movie in 1914 when a local hotel advertised a free cowboy film. She was shocked by the casual prejudice embedded in the movie, which showed heroic American cowboys shooting an old Chinese man, and the lack of discomfort this scene caused the mixed audience. She felt sure that her Hispanic neighbors would have ex-

This 1896 drawing from *Harper's Weekly* portrays the Chinese colony in Mott Street, New York City. *(Library of Congress)*

pressed outrage if the film had depicted unjustified violence directed at a Mexican character. Anna May Wong expressed her own outrage when a man on the street called her a "Chink." Although she had suffered discrimination since elementary school, where her classmates pulled her hair and called her names, it was not until she was seventeen that she worked up enough courage to yell back at that anonymous man on the street.

In response to these kinds of experiences, adolescent immigrants, especially girls, did all they could to make their appearance as American as possible. Chinese teenage girls taped or glued their eyelids to look more American. A worker at the Congressional Mission in San Francisco noted in 1924—with a mixture of approbation and alarm—that "the Chinese girls bob their hair, wear sleeveless dresses, and look just like the little American flappers."[44] Like other adolescent girls in the United States, immigrant girls fought what they considered antiquated norms of dress and respectability. Their struggles to assert their independence were made more difficult by ethnic imperatives of acceptable appearance. For instance, the slenderness that became a cultural ideal for American women during the 1920s directly contradicted Italian parents' ideas about the marital prospects of their daughters, which they believed would suffer if the girls were too thin. Trying to balance conflicting expectations, Italian girls took advantage of the Lenten season to fast and thereby control their weight within a traditional religious framework.

Hairstyles were another contested territory, as short hair seemed unfeminine to many immigrant parents. The first thing Angelita V. did when she married at age nineteen was to bob her hair. Her Mexican father had never permitted her to do so, but she was determined to assert control of her physical appearance to "show my husband that he will not boss me the way my father has done."[45] Like American girls across the country, Angelita refused to relinquish control of the way she looked to any outside authority. Her haircut became a declaration of independence.

Social Life in the Ethnic Community. When taping their eyelids or bobbing their hair or dressing like their peers failed to win immigrant adolescents the acceptance of their peers at school and at work, they retained the option of turning inward for a social life. Social events were common features of immigrant communities. Ethnic social activities functioned as transitional spaces where immigrants could rehearse the American activities of their native-born counterparts but within the safety of familiar company and without fear of exclusion. They also offered alternatives to the highly structured leisure activities encouraged by progressive reformers. Playground reformers, for instance, emphasized team sports for adolescents because they wanted to create a peer dependency they saw as healthier than family connections for the children of benighted immigrants. But reformers were baffled by adolescents' apparent distaste for playground activities running on schedules that prescribed half an hour for patriotic songs, half an hour for supervised "free play," half an hour for track and field, and an hour and a half for team games.

Danish immigrant Marie Eskeren could have explained to them that she would much rather spend her time as she saw fit, typically with peers, as reformers might have wished, but not for the same reasons. Like many of her peers, she sought out people of similar backgrounds for activities of their own design that would both help them act as other American adolescents and reinforce their ethnic ties. Marie enjoyed a community-sponsored Fourth of July event that allowed her to celebrate her new country as well as eat ice cream, picnic, and dance with young men from her old one. She also took trips to amusement parks and beaches with her Danish Sunday School group. In California the second-generation Nisei community organized sports leagues since few adolescent Japanese boys were welcome on school and municipal athletic teams.

As a result of these kinds of activities, though relatively few of the immigrant children who attended language schools continued formal instruction through their adolescence, they retained an ample opportunity for education and social interaction within their communities. In Providence during the early twentieth century, adolescents of all backgrounds participated in sports activities at the Young Federal Hill Athletic Club. But Italian youths flocked to the Dante Alighieri Club, and Jewish teenagers spent time after school or work at the Young Men's and Young Women's Hebrew Associations. The Dante Alighieri Club sponsored classes in both Italian and English, offering a combination of activities designed to promote both Americanization and cultural persistence. All the youth organizations that immigrants frequented provided both literal and

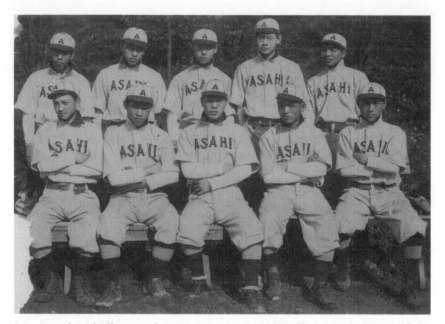

Japanese baseball teams began organizing in Seattle in 1904. Most of the players, like this 1912 Asahi team, were born in Japan. *(University of Washington Libraries)*

figurative space for the kind of balanced acculturation that immigrant adolescents tried to achieve.

An additional motive shaped immigrants' promotion of ethnic social lives: the effort to maintain a measure of control over their sons and daughters. In response to warnings to "keep watch over your adolescent daughter as you did in the Old Country and do not let her go to parties or picnics unattended," community institutions provided numerous social outlets for girls and boys.[46] A few immigrant groups, such as the Mexicans, were particularly stringent about public socializing in supervised settings. Ernesto Galarza attended chaperoned dances where Mexican boys and girls could mingle under strict supervision. In some cases, adolescent Mexicans were so happy to have the opportunity to act like Americans that they were willing to overlook or ignore the supervision. Lucy Acosta, whose mother was a constant presence in her social life, recalled, "I could care less as long as I danced." She considered it more important to have fun than to worry about who was observing her while she did it.[47]

When ethnic communities founded institutions, the emphasis typically tilted toward maintaining tradition. In 1913, for example, the National Slovak Society established a Young Folk's Circle to create enthusiasm for the Slovak language and traditions. In contrast, institutions founded by philanthropists or social workers tended to lean, sometimes heavily, toward Americanization. Young Men's Christian Associations and Young Women's Christian Associations that served largely immigrant populations featured the kinds of activities they considered appropriate for American, Christian young people. The YMCA in a Los Angeles neighborhood populated largely by Nisei took very seriously its mission to provide not only recreation but also missionary activity so that Japanese adolescents could, by becoming Christian, also become more American. But adolescents themselves did not necessarily feel a need to choose one side over another. Plenty of Nisei spent time at the YMCA and also belonged to the Young Men's Buddhist Association. Still, the YMCAs and YWCAs placed such emphasis on the Christian nature of their programs that Jewish communities started Young Men's and Women's Hebrew Associations around the country to provide parallel activities and services.

Adolescents made up an active presence at immigrants' organized social activities. Girls and boys sometimes reacted differently to them. An observer of the Societies of Adolescents, founded to help Polish boys and girls prepare for confirmation, observed that

> Polish boys, who ardently like games, sports, and baseball, as well as loafing around the streets and "chewing tobacco," are not

thrilled to attend the meetings. On the other hand, our adolescent young ladies, although they are also eager to play, do attend meetings more diligently and are more interested in them in general than are their male peers.[48]

Once in attendance at a relatively traditional, ethnically sponsored event, adolescents took control of the social space. During the 1910s, teenagers shocked San Francisco's Chinatown with their public displays of affection at communal picnics and even church events. Similarly, Alma Araiza García and her friends infuriated their chaperones by dancing too closely with their appropriate Mexican partners. They asserted themselves as modern young Americans even within their traditional community settings.

The educators, social workers, employers, and others who played a part in immigrants' lives tried to consider the consequences of adolescents' social and educational choices. Leonard Covello, an immigrant himself, became a public school teacher and then a principal in New York City. He remembered how during his own childhood, "the Italian boy, growing up in the slums of East Harlem and of the lower east side and upper east side of Manhattan, needed the lift that resulted from the recognition of what his people, the Italian people, had created."[49] Covello and other progressive educators believed that while American identity should always come first, ethnic identity need not and should not be erased. It should instead be a source of strength and pride. To that end, Covello started an Italian Club, later called the Italian Circle, at DeWitt Clinton High School. The first group enrolled ambitious boys planning to graduate from high school, attend college, and develop professional careers. As the idea spread to several other New York schools, expanding to include girls at Washington Irving High School, members of the Italian Circle became important figures in the immigrant community. They served as mentors for younger students and worked to convince parents to keep their children in school.

By the early 1920s, Italian Circles at schools all over New York were firmly integrated into their local communities. Attendance at a 1923 Italian Night program by a crowd of adults, adolescents, and children exemplified the most integrated kind of ethnic social life, one rooted in both tradition and modernity. Italian Circle students from several different schools sang vocal selections and recited dramatic pieces in both Italian and English, performed Italian folk dances, and sang patriotic American songs. Here was a communal event that neither suppressed ethnic heritage nor rejected American identity. Other high schools responded to the influx of immigrant students by expanding their language offerings. By 1915 there were 1,965 students studying Scandinavian languages in 54 U.S. high schools, chiefly as a result of the efforts of the Minneapolis-based Society for the Advancement of Scandinavian Study.[50] In this way adolescent immigrants affected their schools and larger communities instead of remaining passive in cultural interchanges.

Dating, Courtship, and Marriage. Socializing with their peers was important for adolescents because some first- and second-generation immigrants married early. No one in their communities protested when Isabella Mendoza married and had her first child at age fifteen, or when Albertina di Grazia married a fellow immigrant from Montazzoli at seventeen. Theoretically, marriage required at least minimal economic security, but with most immigrant adolescents working rather than extending their formal education, youth did not necessarily mean an inability to earn a living. Even if it did, the delay might only be temporary. At seventeen, Peter Kekonnen, a Finnish immigrant, met the fifteen-year-old daughter of Finnish farmers living near the Mesabi Iron Range where he worked as a miner. They waited two years to marry so they could pool their earnings and buy a farm to begin their married lives properly. Early marriage became part of a set of expectations that immigrant girls either embraced or rejected. Italian girls began filling their wedding chests at the age of eight or nine, crocheting lace to trim bed linens and adding sheets, bed covers, and undergarments whenever possible. Most girls' wedding chests were full by the time they were twenty, symbolizing their readiness for marriage. Even Sadie Frowne, a Polish girl in New York who thought that at sixteen she was too young to settle down, would have been worried if she had had no serious suitors.

If the daughters of immigrants delayed marriage, observers took it as a sign of Americanization. This may have been a misreading of some situations, however. When immigrant girls took over their mothers' responsibilities in cases of sickness or death, they became trapped within family responsibilities and married late or not at all. Lucie Cordeau, daughter of French-Canadian immigrants in Lowell, Massachusetts, was sixteen when first her mother and then her older sister died. Working in a textile factory all the while, she took over the household management, becoming "the second mother." This role affected her opportunities for both courtship and marriage as she felt obligated to stay at home until all her younger siblings were out of the house. Even then she had to take care of her father. Few potential spouses were willing to wait. As Lucie recalled with some bitterness, "If you had a boyfriend, when you have to go back home and cook supper for your father or meals for your brothers, the boys never stay long. The friendship never lasts. They say, you take your family before me." Lucie ultimately did marry at age thirty-six, but she always felt she had lost the chances she should have had for adolescent courtship and earlier marriage.[51]

Courtship and marriage became battlegrounds between immigrant parents invested in tradition and children seeking personal autonomy. Even after Lillie Leung started college at Stanford, her parents still clung to the notion that they would find her a husband. As she described the gap between parents and children, "We younger Chinese make fun of the old Chinese idea according to which the parents make all arrangements for the marriage of their children."[52] The modern urban environment separated adults and children in so many ways that it is hardly surprising that adolescents would begin to insist on making their own rules for meeting and spending time with one another. With less intergenerational mingling, traditional systems of chaperonage fell by the wayside. Italian adolescents resisted the traditional practices that had forbidden touching and required courting couples to sit across the table from each other in their parents' homes.

Adolescents took control of their leisure time in a number of ways. For one, they joined pleasure clubs, which organized dances and other social activities. Boys gathered to smoke, drink, and play cards. Girls went in groups to parks and beaches. Pleasure clubs also sponsored dances. Parents may not have thought much of such frivolous activities, but they did prefer group recreation. Maureen Connelly's parents allowed her to participate in the Friends of Irish Freedom in New York under the guise of approving its political aspirations, even though Maureen did not hide the fact that the real purpose of the brief Friday night meetings was the dancing that inevitably followed.

Urban working-class life encouraged the transformation of traditional courtship into modern "dating." Formal calling was not practical when space and privacy were at a premium. Cities offered numerous public spaces where young people could be alone together, such as movie houses, dance halls, and amusement parks. None of these urban spaces was considered sufficiently respectable for middle-class girls during the first years of the twentieth century, but working-class dating practices ultimately diffused up the class ranks. The diffusion was furthered by the growing access of middle-class young men to automobiles, known as "brothels on wheels" by critics who condemned the unsupervised pleasures of dating they offered. Native-born and immigrant parents alike feared the new-found social control exerted by their unruly children.

Immigrant parents found it difficult to accept any middle ground between childhood and adulthood. As their children began to experience adolescence through school, fashion, sports, leisure activities, and courtship or dating, they were forced to confront their limited power over their children's social lives and especially their marital future, even when their children chose to socialize primarily within their ethnic communities. Nonetheless the power of tradition and family ties still shaped the marriage patterns of some immigrant youth. In Greek families, where dowry customs meant that fathers and brothers were responsible for marrying off daughters and sisters, arranged marriages were not uncommon for girls. Greek girls were pressured to marry young because their brothers had to delay or forgo marriage until the sisters were settled. In Chinese immigrant communities the overwhelmingly male population made adolescent girls desirable wives. In 1910 a fourteen-year-old Chinese girl faced a choice between a twenty-year-old man with a large family and a fifty-year-old man living alone. She took her parents' advice and accepted the older man's proposal so that she would not have to serve the younger man's family. The ethnic press discouraged these adolescent marriages, not only for the personal unhappiness that often followed but also for the un-American family patterns they preserved. *L'Italia* reproached Italian men who married teenage girls and Italian parents who encouraged adolescent marriage for hindering the adjustment of the Italian community to America, where, theoretically at least, adolescence was a time for school or work but not marriage.

Immigrant adolescents encountered potential marriage partners in any number of settings. Minnie Kaster met her husband at a shop friend's wedding, and Samuel Lukin married his boss's daughter. By 1919, 85 percent of the students at City College and nearly 30 percent of the students at Hunter College in New York were Jewish, so college mixers furthered the meetings of numerous like-minded young Jewish couples.[53] Like most immigrants, Greek parents placed heavy emphasis on marrying within their own community. Family friends reported to each other if a Greek boy or girl was seen with a non-Greek member of the opposite sex.

Even without such blatant community policing, immigrants and the children of immigrants naturally gravitated in most cases toward dating and marrying people from similar backgrounds. From 1885 to 1920, Danish endogamy rates in Iowa remained at greater than 70 percent.[54] Mexican immigrants took advantage of their geographical flexibility and visited family and friends back home to find husbands and wives and so stay tied to traditional culture. For some groups the high rate of endogamy was less a matter of choice than necessity. With anti-miscegenation laws in effect in California from 1905 to 1948, Japanese, Chinese, and Korean young people had no one to marry but each other. Since each of the groups disdained the others and in some cases regarded them as enemies, cross-national intermarriage among Asians was even more rare than intermarriage among those of Asian and European background.

For all the forces pushing immigrant adolescents to socialize and marry within their own ethnic groups, some pressures worked against them. A serious imbalance between boys and girls within some ethnic groups meant that even if they wanted to marry someone of the same background, some immigrants could not do so. Many Danish communities, for example, particularly in the nineteenth century, were made up mostly of men. As one young Dane wrote home in 1888:

> What we miss most are girls! There are nothing but half-grown children here. There are a lot of old bachelors here just waiting for the girls to get old enough to marry. The innocent lasses don't even celebrate their fifteenth birthday before ten old bachelors in their thirties are on their knees proposing to them. But the girls choose those who have the most gray hair, so there is no point in a young man proposing here.[55]

In such circumstances it is scarcely surprising that at least some young Danish men looked elsewhere for wives. Similarly, young men who emigrated from India typically came without wives and had no opportunity to return home to find them. Some married Mexican women and set up Punjabi-Mexican households where the children spoke English and Spanish and were brought up Catholic but had godparents who were also Punjabi-Mexican couples.

Even young men who claimed to want American-born or thoroughly Americanized wives still valued some attachment to a shared set of ethnic and cultural values. They looked within their communities for the attributes they wanted or needed most. Clara Corica believed that she received "at least a dozen marriage proposals because I could be useful to 'guys' and 'racketeers.'"[56] In her Italian neighborhood in Cleveland, the fact that Clara was a high school teacher made her seem overly educated and ambitious to some men but ironically imbued her with a status and fluency in American society that made her seem desirable to the criminal types who valued her skills and knowledge.

In their choice of peers from similar backgrounds as spouses, adolescents took one of the most important steps toward adulthood in likeminded company. Most of them had grown up trying to find the delicate balance between tradition and modernity. They had been compelled by both family and community necessity and personal choice to adapt to American society and culture without completely forsaking their ethnic heritage. As they prepared to start families, they sought others with similar experiences to join them in the enterprise of raising the next generation of children, whose American identities would be more secure but whose ethnic identities would emerge from a whole new set of challenges.

CHAPTER FIVE

After the Door Closed: The Effects of Restrictive Legislation and the Depression

---

🌿 ALL THE generally important changes in late-nineteenth- and early-twentieth-century American life also reshaped the world of immigrant children. The United States had completed its transformation to an urban industrial society, with all the adjustments that entailed. After the political turmoil of the 1890s, the country had settled into a period of relative political stability on the national level and serious reform at the state and local levels. By the end of World War I the nation had demonstrated its critical importance to global politics and economics and had clearly become the preeminent industrial powerhouse, a status with a real impact on working-class Americans.

By the mid-1920s, much had changed in immigrant life as well. Travel to America took less time, cost less, and was more organized a process than in 1880. Immigrants who had been in the United

States for a period of time took advantage of widespread, if limited, economic advancement and moved out of the worst housing in decaying city centers. The growth of municipal mass-transit systems made it easier for them to travel to and from jobs over a wider area. They purchased modest homes in cities and suburbs and expanded their farm holdings in the countryside. Indoor plumbing was much more common, and indoor electricity and telephones were becoming regular fixtures of city life. Progressive Era reform ameliorated some of the worst living conditions, even for those who stayed behind in urban centers. Ethnic fragmentation remained common, but immigrant children who had grown up in America cooperated in certain venues, particularly in organized labor.

Perhaps most important for immigrants was the fact that by the mid-1920s at least one generation, and in some cases two generations, of immigrant children had grown up in America. No longer were all ethnic Americans recent arrivals. A high percentage of them were U.S. citizens by simple right of birth, which gave immigrant communities expanded confidence in dealing with American life. That confidence became increasingly necessary after World War I, when a series of legislative restrictions sharply limited the numbers of immigrants allowed to enter the United States. Despite the coming-of-age of many immigrants and the new restrictions, there remained a sizable cohort of immigrant children well into the 1930s. The children who immigrated before the restrictive legislation took effect, as well as the children born during the later 1920s and the 1930s to the most recent immigrants, continued to face the same clash of cultures that their predecessors had dealt with decades earlier. As a result of newly stabilized ethnic populations and the economic crisis of the Great Depression, this last generation of immigrant children confronted altered circumstances, but the story is not complete without a general consideration of their experiences.

Restrictive Immigration Legislation

At first World War I seemed to present immigrants with a golden opportunity to demonstrate their loyalty to the country that had taken them in. Most immigrants and their children responded enthusiastically to calls for economic and labor support. Thousands of immigrants served in the U.S. military. Their participation was recognized, but the never-dormant nativism embedded in American culture blossomed. Since as many as a third of American troops were foreign-born or the children of immigrants, the government decided to combine military training with intense Americanization programs. Meanwhile, on the home front, suspicion of all things foreign intensified. Ostensibly patriotic campaigns removed German (and sometimes other languages) from high school and college curricula, banned performances of musical works by German composers, and made all those with foreign names suspect of disloyalty and treason. Because the bulk of German immigration had occurred in the nineteenth century, this meant that third- and fourth-generation Americans of German descent now experienced the kind of prejudice they themselves had levied against the "new immigrants" of the late nineteenth and early twentieth centuries.

The aftermath of World War I brought a new host of problems to immigrant communities. Anti-German sentiment spilled over into a more generalized xenophobia. Urban immigrants found themselves in increasing—and increasingly violent—conflict with African Americans, whose great migration to the cities during and after the war led to constant competition with the poorest immigrants over housing and jobs. Major riots in Chicago and Tulsa, among other places, were products of racial and ethnic contention. Meanwhile rural immigrant farmers, who had enjoyed the heyday of American agriculture in the preceding decade, now found themselves confronting a dramatic agricultural depression from which

The federal government encouraged immigrant contributions to the World War I fund-raising effort, as in this 1917 poster. *(Library of Congress)*

there seemed to be no escape. All these issues limited the opportunities of the many thousands of immigrants who came to the United States after the brief hiatus dictated by the exigencies of war.

Anti-immigration forces in the United States regarded the renewal of immigration with horror. They had hoped the war would put an end to the influx, especially given the economic recession immediately following the end of hostilities. But within a few years the U.S. industrial machine was once again in full motion, and immigrants could find employment easily. The Immigration Restriction League, in existence since 1894, swung into action. Although it had always attracted a solid membership, including many intellectuals and social elites, by 1920 the organization could count on a whole new range of allies. Leaders of the American Federation of Labor craft unions continued to resent unskilled immigrant labor, especially after successful open-shop campaigns during the early 1900s. Prohibitionists denounced the saloon culture embedded in immigrant life. Eugenicists and promoters of scientific racism spread the idea of a global hierarchy of races, with the United States threatened by the constant influx of "inferior" races of Slavs, Japanese, and Mexicans. Even Progressives like Theodore Roosevelt cautioned against "race suicide," urging white middle-class women to have more children in order to preserve the nation's racial integrity. A revamped Ku Klux Klan, targeting Jews and Catholics as well as African Americans, fought bitterly against the travesties of modern culture for which it blamed foreigners. Automobile manufacturer Henry Ford, the most admired man in America, made explicit anti-Semitism acceptable in his popular newspaper, the *Dearborn Independent*.

Earlier anti-immigration efforts had met with limited success since the passage of the Chinese Exclusion Act in 1882, especially as it was clear to many industrialists that immigrant labor was vital for economic growth. Several attempts to impose a literacy test on immigrants failed, though generally due to presidential veto rather than congressional or popular opposition. Before World War I, pro-immigrant forces had successfully adopted the progressive tactic of forming commissions to issue reports. The 1911 Dillingham Commission's multi-volume report, which cemented the perceived difference between "old" and "new" immigrants, was replete with stereotypical and even racist assumptions about immigrants but nonetheless suggested no restrictive legislation other than a literacy test, which was again vetoed.

After a war that rhetorically elevated "100 percent American-ism" to new heights, and a postwar Red Scare that identified bolshevism with foreign radicals corrupting America from the inside, popular sentiment for immigration restriction was easily galvanized.

Turmoil in the wake of the Russian and Mexican revolutions, not to mention the ongoing fallout from World War I, seemed to be fomenting even more immigration. In these circumstances Albert Johnson, a Republican congressman from Washington, argued that an emergency measure was needed to prevent millions of refugees of war and revolution from pouring into the United States. In 1921 the Emergency Immigration Act limited immigration to small quotas based on the population of each nationality in the 1910 census and limited overall immigration from Europe to approximately 350,000 a year. President Woodrow Wilson opposed such legislation, but his successor Warren Harding signed it and also approved a two-year extension in 1922.

For the next few years a heated debate over immigration restriction raged in both popular and political discourse. Anti-immigrant advocates warned that immigrants' foreign ideas would poison the body politic. They claimed that the new immigrants, unlike the old, arrived with no plans to become loyal American citizens and instead insisted on living (and voting) in blocs, creating pockets of un-American life throughout the country. They blamed immigrants for working for such low wages that they undermined the true Americans' ability to earn a living. Those who favored immigration argued that by participating in the war, the United States had made a commitment to the people of the world that it could not abandon by refusing refugees entrance. They responded to the fear of radicalism by pointing out that ideas know no borders or exclusion in a free society. Ethnic groups issued reports demonstrating that the remarkable industrial, social, and scientific progress of the United States in recent decades had been due largely to the manpower and brainpower of the new immigrants. Yet the nativist perspective, trumping facts and logic, prevailed at almost every turn.

Given the mythology of the United States as a land of freedom and refuge, even the most ardent immigration restrictionists did not believe they could achieve a complete moratorium on immigration. In fact they supported the continuing immigration of the supposedly superior British, Scandinavian, and—despite the World War I experience—German immigrants. The solution came in the form of the 1924 National Origins Act. This legislation established quotas based on the 1890 United States Census, which did not yet reflect the masses of "undesirables" arriving in the United States. Under the new law, immigrants would receive certificates of entry before departing their native lands, so as to prevent confusion at American ports of entry. The total number of immigrants to be allowed each year was cut to approximately 160,000. The law also excluded all immigrants ineligible to become citizens, a measure aimed at the Japanese and Koreans. The bill passed Congress with overwhelming majorities and remained the basic framework for U.S. immigration policy until the 1960s.

Ethnic groups in the United States protested to no avail. Even the indignation of foreign governments, particularly that of Japan, which had previously cooperated with the U.S. government on immigration policy, occasioned no apology or response. U.S. foreign policy did not immediately change as a result of the 1924 legislation, but it had other consequences. The Japanese population in the United States feared for the legal status of even American-born Nissei, a fear confirmed by the internment policies enacted during World War II. Although restrictionists could not have foreseen the coming plight of the Jews in Europe, hundreds of thousands of Jews who would likely have emigrated to America were instead murdered during the Holocaust. Because of exemptions for the Western Hemisphere in both the Emergency Immigration Act and the National Origins Act, Canadians and Mexicans continued to emigrate. Half a million Mexicans entered the United States during the 1920s, filling jobs in commercial agriculture, mining, and the steel and automobile industries. They ultimately became the majority of the population in cities like San Antonio and Los Angeles.

Implementation and enforcement of immigration restriction gradually affected all immigrants, whether children or not. If only a few family members had settled in the United States, the remaining family back home might have been able to exploit certain loopholes to gain their own admission. In many cases, though, quotas were strictly enforced, and families were broken up by the new legislation. Without a stream of recent immigrants pouring into ethnic communities, ethnic institutions gradually became harder to maintain. With return migration basically over and fewer immigrants sending money overseas for family members' passage, the links between the Old and New Worlds became somewhat more tenuous for European and Asian communities. Holidays and particularly traditional foods became even more important in holding on to traditional customs as they were both easily reproducible and easily accommodated to American norms. During the period of mass immigration, immigrant children had typically believed that their future success depended on their ability to acculturate. Once restrictive legislation took effect, even the most traditional elements of ethnic communities generally concentrated on feeling at home in America, essentially following the paths already blazed by their own children.

Immigration restrictions had political and economic repercussions too. From the mid-1920s on, the Democratic party became ever more firmly the political party of most immigrants' choice. The Republican party's big-business interests and prohibitionist leanings had never appealed to most immigrants, especially those who lived in cities, but Democratic leaders like Al Smith, the first Catholic to run for president of the United States, now earned the undying commitment of working-class ethnic communities. The Committee of Industrial Unions (later the Congress of Industrial Organizations, the CIO), founded within the American Federation of Labor to organize unskilled workers in mass-production industries, succeeded in part because interethnic conflict had waned considerably. Not all immigrant children, now grown, or second-generation immigrants got along with one another. Plenty of prejudice continued. Yet the closed borders required immigrants committed to

American life to recognize the similar goals held by nearly all ethnic communities and to work together for economic justice. In the 1930s these political and economic trends reached their zenith in the New Deal Democratic coalition under Franklin Roosevelt.

The enthusiasm with which native-born Americans welcomed restriction frightened many immigrants. Their protests received little publicity and achieved virtually nothing. Immigrant children, either growing up during this period or raising their own children, generally concluded that rapid acculturation was the swiftest path toward acceptance. As a result, some of the means by which tradition had been preserved weakened noticeably in the late 1920s and early 1930s. Enrollment in language schools dropped sharply. Children might still learn their heritage language at home, but the formal setting of language schools began to strike some immigrants as somehow un-American. The balance of writing in ethnic newspapers shifted to English. Settlement houses and social workers ministering to immigrants suffered greatly for lack of funding. Mutual aid societies lingered on, but they lost communal centrality as the deepening depression left private philanthropic efforts powerless in comparison to government programs. Depression-era rhetoric about the need for all Americans to pull together in a time of crisis papered over the ethnic diversity of the American population (though it was less effective for racial diversity). Immigrants who had been caught between two worlds during their own childhood now cast their lots on the side of Americanization, regardless of how they might have negotiated their own identities as children and adolescents. One indication of the shift was the slow but steady rise of ethnic intermarriage rates among second- and third-generation immigrants.

The Depression and Childhood in Immigrant Communities

The depression played a critical role in the experience of immigrant children after mass immigration ended. They had dealt with economic hard times before. Relatively few had known real economic security while growing up, though many had found increasing stability as their families adjusted to American life. The cyclical nature of the American economy, exemplified by the Panic of 1893 and the recession immediately after World War I, had affected all Americans adversely. But the all-encompassing nature of the depression, which lasted more than a decade, hit hard immigrant children's opportunities to secure a better life or to offer a better life to their own children. Elements of ethnic and working-class culture might have prepared them for the spirit of moral and social cooperation that characterized the depression era for many Americans. Still, the communal ethic could not protect them from economic privation and the deleterious effects of scarcity. For both children and cultural ideas about childhood, the depression turned out to be a pivotal period that overlapped with the aftereffects of restrictive legislation on immigrant and ethnic life.

African Americans were the last hired and first fired for most depression-era jobs, but people with accents perceived as foreigners fared little better. Immigrants who had begun their American lives as farmers often lost their farms and were forced to join the unemployed masses in cities. In California a federal policy deported Mexicans back to Mexico. This repatriation policy, ironic in light of the fact that Mexico had been excluded from immigration restriction in order to assure commercial agricultural interests of a constant supply of cheap labor, demonstrated Mexicans' fragile status. Roosevelt's New Deal policies reduced the number of forced repatriations, but by then families had been separated and children's education disrupted. Those Mexicans who remained in the United States faced a discrimination that only solidified their commitment to a distinctly Mexican-American ethnic identity, rooted partly in joining American labor unions and fighting for a Mexican-American brand of social justice. The poorest segment of the Japanese population in America also returned home during the depression, though Japanese landowners often held on to their land. In general, Asian immigrants were excluded from New Deal programs since they were ineligible for citizenship, though children born in the United States could theoretically benefit. They found the steadiest work in ethnic enterprises, which, as in the Mexican case, actually reinforced communal solidarity. Overall, immigrants continued to deploy the strategies they had always used in the past for finding jobs and housing, but America now presented fewer opportunities for advancement.

The most immediately evident change in children's experience was the increasing numbers of families sinking into poverty. The past decades had not brought equal distribution of wealth or financial security to all Americans, but the expansion of industrial and manufacturing jobs and the growing dominance of the United States on the world stage had consistently made upward social mobility a realistic possibility for poor working families. With few exceptions, American industry suffered grievously from the depression. Layoffs became so common that few workers could count on either longevity or skill to preserve their jobs. Unemployment rates soared, wages plummeted. Rather than advancement, family survival became the goal.

Whereas in previous years children's paid work had made up the economic gap in poor families, during the depression the rate of child labor fell precipitously. Putting children to work was widely perceived as taking jobs away from unemployed adult men willing to accept any and all kinds of work. For example, networks of newsboys collapsed as men took over their jobs. With few regulations on wages, especially during the early years of the depression, the low pay of jobs previously performed by children did not deter adults desperate to make even a little money. Feeling ran so high against children "stealing" what could be the rightful wages of adults that even gender conventions were overturned. In many poor families, women became the primary or secondary breadwinners instead of their husbands or children. Other factors prompted this shift: many men refused to demean themselves by taking on jobs associated with women, such as domestic and laundry work, but children's work held less of a stigma. The end result was that families were far more likely to depend on women's and men's jobs, if they could find them, than on children's labor. Only on family farms did children's work continue to play a vital role in the family economy. But because children's agricultural labor had almost never been counted in statistical assessments of the rates of child labor, statistics were unaffected by the continuation of children's farm work.

The sharp reduction in child labor led to other changes in children's lives. Work and education, as always, operated on something of an inverse scale. More American children than ever before attended and stayed in school. Education was free and no longer cost anything in terms of missing wages, since urban children were so much less likely to work. In the late 1920s, public schools had a temporary respite from overcrowding as restrictive legislation reduced the numbers of newcomers; but throughout the 1930s classrooms overflowed with children staying in school rather than entering the labor force. Many of these children tried to pick up odd jobs and earn cash whenever they could, but school rather than work became the chief concern of most American children, regardless of background.

The numbers of children attending school grew at all levels nationwide, but the largest growth was at the high school level. By the 1920s high school attendance had become a fairly common experience for middle-class adolescents, but the depression marked the first time in American history that most adolescents went to high school. Removed from the economic arena by force, they found high schools an acceptable and, as it turned out, transformative destination. The consequences of widespread secondary schooling were many. For one, American adolescents became the most highly educated in the industrial world. This was evident during World War

II, when, in sharp contrast to the many illiterate American soldiers in 1917–1918, American servicemen and women who had grown up during the depression constituted the best-educated military force in history. Another consequence of widespread secondary schooling was the cementing of a distinct youth culture. This process had been ongoing for some time and owed its origins in part to the growth in middle-class high school attendance from the Civil War onward. Another factor contributing to the development of youth culture was the experience of immigrant children and adolescents, who often found more in common with their peers than with their "old-fashioned" parents. Now that more and more adolescents of all backgrounds were spending so much time together in high schools, in spaces removed from their families, where success reinforced peer culture rather than family ties, adolescence took on a whole new shape. By going to high school, immigrant adolescents had just as much chance to be a part of youth culture as their native-born peers did.

Prejudice did not disappear overnight, and high schools remained places where discrimination played a role. The vast majority of American high schools were segregated. Asian students in some states still found themselves excluded. But during the period of national economic emergency class background mattered less than it once had, and by the mid-1930s relatively few high school students, with the important exception of Mexicans, had been born abroad.

This confluence of factors made high schools not only sites of acculturation for immigrants, as they had been in the past, but also centers for the homogenization of youth culture. Adolescent modes of dress, speech, and recreation exerted a strong influence on both current high school students and those who aspired to join them. Peer pressure encouraged adolescents to prioritize friends over family, and many students spent more time in and out of school with peers than with their families. Youth culture rarely led adolescents to cut all family ties. Their economic dependency on their families generally increased during the depression. But for millions of immigrant adolescents, high school now offered the smoothest, most enjoyable assurance of acceptance in America. That secondary education continued to hold out the promise of increased economic opportunity expanded its appeal to students and parents alike.

Youth culture depended on shared experiences, such as high school education, but also on shared goods. Ironically, a time of economic deprivation also saw a rise in certain kinds of consumerism, which proved to be another path toward American identity for immigrant children and adolescents. Commercial entertainment exploded in popularity during the depression. Virtually every household in America owned a radio, which was both an object and a provider of consumerism. Millions of Americans listened not only to President Roosevelt's fireside chats but also to entertainment programming and advertisements that brought cultural icons like *Amos & Andy* and consumer products like Iodent toothpaste to the masses. Some of these programs cut across various social dividing lines. *The Rise of the Goldbergs* chronicled the acculturation process of a supposedly typical Jewish family in ways that also appealed to families of other ethnic backgrounds, and offered material aimed at both parents and children. Other radio programs, like *The Shadow*, primarily targeted children. Movies too grew immensely popular during the depression. Seeking escape from their troubles and a relatively cheap entertainment, millions of Americans flocked to movie theaters in towns and cities across the United States. Much as high school social life did for adolescents, movies set standards for everything from popular dances to clothing styles to dating etiquette. The social realism of some depression-era movies attracted large crowds, but for immigrant children and adolescents, movie theaters became another kind of school in which they could learn how to dress, think, and act like Americans. Child stars like Shirley Temple provided direct models of the rewards that would come to those who knew how to act appropriately.

Widespread social acceptance of youth culture was reflected both in the actual experiences of children and adolescents and in conceptions of childhood. As the rate of child labor declined, even working-class families could adopt an understanding of childhood as a protected stage of life during which children should be shielded from economic responsibility and be left free to develop. The right to childhood defended so vigorously by progressive reformers seemed more and more attainable, though no one would have wished for the drastic economic realignments that made it so. Federal policy toward childhood and youth actualized these earlier ideas. The Children's Bureau lobbied hard for programs to consider the needs of children, in 1933 sponsoring a conference that led to the Child Health and Recovery Program.

Once Roosevelt assumed the presidency in 1933, his patchwork of New Deal programs often included and sometimes targeted youth. Federal funding provided for Emergency Day Nurseries, which significantly increased the number of children attending preschool. First the Civil Works Administration and then the Works Progress Administration oversaw the construction of schools, playgrounds, parks, swimming pools, and athletic fields, all of which improved the physical environment of children's lives while serving larger communities as well. The Works Progress Administration also made federal funding available for school lunch programs that supplied many children with their only full meal of the day. Beginning in 1933, the Civilian Conservation Corps enrolled thousands of boys and young men in projects such as clearing forests or conserving federal lands. Participation in the Civilian Conservation Corps typically meant living in special work camps and earning a small but steady wage, both features that appealed to boys looking to reduce the drain on their families.

The National Youth Administration included girls as well as boys, with educational and vocational programs designed to keep adolescents in school, teach them practical job skills, and prepare them for eventual transition to adult employment. Some immigrant adolescents found National Youth Administration programs particularly helpful because they could learn the middle-class values, behavioral norms, and family-life skills that would solidify their sense of belonging in America.

Finally, the Social Security Act of 1935 included some of the farthest-reaching and longest-lasting provisions for children. The law formalized the definition of dependent children and mandated a combination of state and federal funding for children with special needs, needy mothers and children, and dependent children that today still exists in one form or another. The institutionalization of childhood as a stage of dependency, whether on family or government, represented the culmination of a major shift from earlier ideas about the economic value of children. As a result of both restrictive legislation and the depression, immigrant families took part in this major social change and thereby moved another step closer to constructing an American identity.

CHAPTER SIX

Immigrant Children
and Modern America

✒ THE PHENOMENON of mass immigration during the late nineteenth and early twentieth centuries fundamentally shaped both the modern United States and the millions of immigrants who crossed oceans and borders to live there. In a way, American history during this era replicated the experiences of immigrant children. A time of uncertainty and hardship was followed by a period of adjustment, punctuated by reversals of fortune, that generally led to at least modest success and sometimes great triumph. Like immigrants, other Americans were also reluctant to jettison all their traditions and gradually found ways to accommodate themselves to their new environment without leaving behind every element of the past. Old traditions took on new forms in a process of modernization, with far-reaching effects. Disputes between generations fostered a certain amount of bitterness and upheaval but were resolved to some extent by shared values and aspirations. Various groups of people learned to live with one another.

As this book should make clear, there was no singular immigrant experience, though there were certain commonalities in immigrant life. That was true even within ethnic groups, let alone across groups of immigrants from places as varied as Japan, Canada, Mexico, Italy, Norway, Poland, and Germany, among others. It is critical to pay attention to differences. Danes who moved to farms in the Upper Midwest, accepted immediately as superior white stock, shared few experiences with Chinese "paper sons" who entered the United States through a legal loophole, worked primarily as unskilled laborers in the West, and set up families slowly, if at all. Urban/rural, skilled/unskilled, literate/illiterate, white/racially "other"—all these dichotomies and many more differences mattered deeply in shaping immigrant life. Yet there were important similarities as well. Economic opportunity was the single most crucial motive for all groups involved in mass immigration. The challenge of balancing Old World tradition with New World expectations loomed large for all of them, no matter how eager they were to establish themselves as bona fide Americans. And the difficulty of raising children, or of growing up, in an environment that undermined the social reproduction of traditional family life confronted immigrants across boundaries of ethnicity, nationality, and race. Immigrant children shared a great deal.

Even when these children lived in heavily ethnic communities or neighborhoods, their experiences with education, work, play, and even discrimination exposed them to a diversity of interests that shaped their childhood. Because children met and mingled in their own spaces, in schools, on playgrounds and streets, they frequently had more opportunities than their parents to broaden their ideas about what it meant to live in America and become American. At the same time that a cadre of educators and social workers insisted on transformative education, many immigrant children consciously recognized what made them Jewish, or Mexican, or Sicilian, and made choices about how—or whether—to maintain their ethnic identities.

For all these reasons, one can see certain structural similarities in immigrants' experiences and in the lives of their children, who had the twin burdens of living as symbols and as individuals. It would be an overstatement to say that similarity outweighed difference, but it would be equally misleading to claim that cultural specificity trumped all the other factors shaping immigrant children's lives. A more balanced approach explores and appreciates both similarity and difference in immigrant children's lives. Where an elementary school classroom in a large urban area in 1900 might contain fifty students from thirty different backgrounds, all living in the same neighborhood and attending the same school and learning from the same teacher, it would be absurd to deny the shared experiences. But it would be equally problematic to deny that the children of Asian descent would experience more discrimination, or that the well-meaning teacher probably assumed that the Jewish and German children would do better work than the Polish and Italian children, or that a boy might have to go to work next month but a girl would stay in school just because she could not earn as much.

Certain motifs, like education and gender, recur throughout the history of immigrant children and provide rich ground for investigating their similarities and differences. Exploring the education of immigrant children opens a window into a central theme of American history: the question of how individuals from traditional groups navigate between the twin shoals of cultural retention and cultural adaptation. Education of all kinds mediated immigrants' experiences in turn-of-the-century America. Immigrant children and adolescents' encounters with expanding educational opportunities embodied the central tension between tradition and modernity in their lives. Those opportunities took many forms and affected immigrant children in a variety of ways. As sites of individual learning, peer socialization, and youth culture, public schools, particularly in the urban areas that were home to large concentrations of immigrants, played a defining role in introducing immigrants to idealized versions of American society and culture that often proved irresistible to children and adolescents longing to fit in. At the same time the increasing variety of curriculums made possible by swelling school populations led to the imposition of expectations based on class, gender, and race, especially on the growing numbers of secondary school students. Many immigrant children were not afforded the luxury of standardized formal schooling; for them, alternative forms of education such as clubs, evening classes, and periodicals served an important educational function. Virtually all these educational experiences tended to move immigrant students toward a modernization defined in part by their own willingness to learn to be American youth. In public school classrooms, *barrio* youth clubs, and church and synagogue basements, children learned lessons, sometimes pleasurable and sometimes painful, about Old World expectations and New World demands.

Like education, debates about gender provided another foundation for immigrant children's lives. To some degree the experience of immigration may have encouraged conservative tendencies in immigrant parents. They believed that the very act of setting out for parts unknown was in itself radical enough; as little else as possible should change in their lives beyond the basic expansion of opportunity. Of course the expansion of opportunity itself inevitably brought with it significant change. The generation gap so noticeable between parents and children owed something to the adults' interest in maintaining a social and cultural continuity that would counterbalance the deeply foreign nature of their new environment. Policing the proper roles of boys and girls provided one outlet for these conservative tendencies—a relatively easy outlet given that the dominant middle-class culture of America also distinguished sharply between boys and girls. Immigrants assumed they would be judged both by their ethnic peers and their outside observers for their children's behavior. Therefore they emphasized conserving their own heritage to ensure what they considered appropriate behavior. Children, under heavy external pressure to jettison traditional modes of life for modern, American norms, found themselves caught between implacable forces when they perceived their parents' conservatism increasing in direct proportion to their own willingness to change their way of life.

Despite its contested nature, gender eventually became a conciliatory force. The Americanization movement gradually convinced immigrants of all ethnic and national origins that middle-class gender ideology, especially the separation of home and work, was a prerequisite for American citizenship and acceptance. The pervasiveness of distinct gender roles across ethnicity and even class meant that girls of all backgrounds and boys of all backgrounds automatically shared a bond and basis for understanding. During the late nineteenth and early twentieth centuries, immigrant adolescents could lift their families into higher social and cultural spheres by emulating the gender identity of idealized adolescents. Their behavior reflected on their families and influenced their integration into American society, an integration few immigrants dismissed as unnecessary or undesirable. As students, workers, family members, consumers, and church or synagogue members, immigrant adolescents found that expectations based on their gender played a key role in their acculturation into American life.

The consideration of the opportunities, options, and constraints of a century ago should contribute an important historical context to current debates over immigrant children. The specific cast of characters has changed, but in many ways the social script has not. Now, as then, immigrant children face the hostility of an increasingly unwelcoming American public. Now, as then, that hostility is frequently concentrated on schools and education policy. Now, as then, immigrant children walk a fine line between pride in retaining their particular heritage and satisfaction in adapting to the dominant culture. Now, as then, various forms of education are the prime mediators of most immigrant children's formative experiences in America. Immigration remains as central to the formation and evolution of the United States in the present as it has been in the past.

As both real people and symbols, turn-of-the-century immigrant children played a vital role. Their labor contributed to the unprecedented productivity and economic growth of their new country. Their relationships with family members, teachers, employers, representatives of the state, and reformers provided the basis for Progressive Era reform and ultimately, some historians believe, for the rise of the welfare state during the New Deal. Their ability to strike a balance, however uneasy, between the Old World and the New yielded a heterogeneous American society characterized by diverse cultural forms as well as shared values. Their very presence irrevocably altered ideas about childhood and youth in the modern world. Their story *is* the story of the United States during one of the pivotal moments in the nation's history.

Notes

Chapter 1. Childhood and Immigrants

1. Cyrus H. McCormick, "Introductory Remarks," 1911, in James Marten, ed., *Childhood and Child Welfare in the Progressive Era: A Brief History with Documents* (Boston: Bedford/St. Martin's, 2005), 124–125.
2. Charles Hirschman, "Immigration and the American Century," *Demography* 42 (November 2005): 596–597.

Chapter 2. The Landscape of Early Childhood

1. Jacob A. Riis, *How the Other Half Lives* (Boston: Bedford/St. Martin's, 1996 [original ed. 1890]), 148.
2. Quoted in Lawrence H. Fuchs, *The American Kaleidoscope: Race, Ethnicity, and the Civic Culture* (Hanover, N.H.: Wesleyan University Press, 1990), 115.
3. Quoted in David G. Gutiérrez, *Walls and Mirrors: Mexican Americans, Mexican Immigrants, the Politics of Ethnicity* (Berkeley: University of California Press, 1995), 55.
4. T. J. Woofter, Jr., *Race and Ethnic Groups in American Life* (New York: McGraw Hill, 1933), 12–21.
5. Quoted in George J. Sánchez, *Becoming Mexican American: Ethnicity, Culture, and Identity in Chicano Los Angeles, 1900–1945* (New York: Oxford University Press, 1993), 82.
6. Emily Greene Balch, *Our Slavic Fellow Citizens* (New York: Charities Publication Committee, 1910), 330–331.
7. Edith Abbott, *The Tenements of Chicago, 1908–1935* (Chicago: University of Chicago Press, 1936), 490.

8. Valdemar Wahl, Grand Falls, to his parents, November 6, 1883, in Frederick Hale, ed., *Danes in North America* (Seattle: University of Washington Press, 1984), 51.

9. Joan M. Jensen, "The Death of Rosa: Sexuality in Rural America," *Agricultural History* 67 (Fall 1993): 1–12.

10. Emma Duke, "Infant Mortality: Results of a Field Study in Johnstown, Pennsylvania," 1913, in Robert H. Bremner, ed., *Children and Youth in America: A Documentary History*, Vol. II: *1866–1923* (Cambridge: Harvard University Press, 1971), 969–971.

11. Quoted in Judy Yung, *Chinese Women of America: A Pictorial History* (Seattle: University of Washington Press, 1986), 10.

12. Quoted in Edmund DeS. Brunner, *Immigrant Farmers and Their Children* (Garden City: Doubleday, Doran and Co., 1929), 216.

13. Quoted in Mario T. Garcia, "La Familia: The Mexican Immigrant Family, 1900–1930," in Mario Barrera, Alberto Camarillo, and Francisco Hernandez, eds., *Work, Family, Sex Roles, Language: The National Association for Chicano Studies, Selected Papers, 1979* (Berkeley: Tonatiuh-Quinto Sol, 1980), 125.

14. Ernest Poole, "The Lung Block," 1903, in Bremner, *Children and Youth in America*, Vol. II: *1866–1923*, 886–888.

15. Gerard J. Brault, *The French-Canadian Heritage in New England* (Hanover, N.H.: University Press of New England, 1986), 60.

16. Home Missionary Society of the City of Philadelphia, Visiting Book, 1880–1889, Collection 3036, Historical Society of Pennsylvania.

17. John Bodnar, *The Transplanted: A History of Immigrants in Urban America* (Bloomington: Indiana University Press, 1985), 77.

18. Brunner, *Immigrant Farmers and Their Children*, 221.

19. Niles Carpenter, *Immigrants and Their Children, 1920* (Washington, D.C.: Government Printing Office, 1927), 202.

20. Roger Daniels, *Guarding the Golden Door: American Immigration Policy and Immigrants Since 1882* (New York: Hill & Wang, 2004), 25.

21. Walter E. Kruesi, "The School of Outdoor Life for Tuberculous Children," 1909, in Marten, *Childhood and Child Welfare in the Progressive Era*, 99–102.

22. Ernesto Galarza, *Barrio Boy* (Notre Dame: University of Notre Dame Press, 1971), 255.

23. Quoted in Richard A. Meckel, *Save the Babies: American Public Health Reform and the Prevention of Infant Mortality, 1850–1929* (Baltimore: Johns Hopkins University Press, 1990), 131.

24. A. G. Toth, "How We Should Live in America," 1899, in Wayne Moquin, ed., *Makers of America: Natives and Aliens, 1891–1903* (New York: Encyclopaedia Britannica Educational Corp., 1971), 243.

25. Riis, *How the Other Half Lives*, 88.

26. Kate Simon, *Bronx Primitive: Portraits in a Childhood* (New York: Penguin, 1982), 68–70.

27. Ford H. Kuramoto, *A History of the Shonien, 1914–1927: An Account of a Program of Institutional Care of Japanese Children in Los Angeles* (San Francisco: R. and E. Research Associates, 1976), 10–15.

28. Rose Carini interview, "An Oral History of the Italians in Milwaukee," Part 2, *Children in Urban America Project* (hereafter CUAP), <http://xserver1.its.mu.edu/2856446298815.hsp> (January 25, 2006).

29. Bill Hosokawa, *Out of the Frying Pan: Reflections of a Japanese American* (Niwot, Colo.: University Press of Colorado, 1998), 1.

30. Richard W. Gilder, "The Kindergarten: An Uplifting Social Influence in the Home and the District," 1903, in Bremner, *Children and Youth in America*, Vol. II: *1866–1923*, 1459–1460; Kathleen Kaufman and Dianne Knorr, "By Foot, by Horse, by Crummy: Louise Van Ee, School Nurse in Bingham Canyon, 1921–1939," *Utah Historical Quarterly* 69 (Winter 2001): 50.

31. Americanization Division, Bureau of Education, "Americanization Through the Kindergarten," 1919, in Bremner, *Children and Youth in America*, Vol. II: *1866–1923*, 1460–1462.

Chapter 3. At School, at Work, at Home, at Play

1. Ernesto Galarza, "Barrio Boy," in Gordon Hutner, ed., *Immigrant Voices: Twenty-Four Narratives on Becoming an American* (New York: Signet Classics, 1999), 356.

2. John E. Bodnar, "Socialization and Adaptation: Immigrant Families in Scranton, 1880–1890," *Pennsylvania History* 43 (April 1976): 158.

3. Orest Subtelny, *Ukrainians in North America: An Illustrated History* (Toronto: University of Toronto Press, 1991), 24.

4. Mike Taje quoted in Ronald D. Cohen, *Children of the Mill: Schooling and Society in Gary, Indiana, 1906–1960* (Bloomington: Indiana University Press, 1990), 10.

5. Mary Lyons-Barrett, "Child Labor in the Early Sugar Beet Industry in the Great Plains, 1890–1920," *Great Plains Quarterly* 25 (Winter 2005): 29–31.

6. Maurice Hindus, *Green Worlds: An Informal Chronicle* (New York: Doubleday, Doran & Co., 1938), 98.
7. Leonard Dinnerstein, Roger L. Nichols, and David M. Reimers, *Natives and Strangers: A Multicultural History of Americans* (New York: Oxford University Press, 1996), 147.
8. Pennsylvania Child Labor Committee, *The Working Child and the Law* (n.p., 1922), 16.
9. Selma C. Berrol, "School Days on the Old East Side: The Italian and Jewish Experience," *New York History* 57 (April 1976): 210–213.
10. Bodnar, *The Transplanted*, 77.
11. Gilbert C. González, "Women, Work, and Community in the Mexican *Colonias* of the Southern California Citrus Belt," in Manuel G. Gonzales and Cynthia M. Gonzales, eds., *En Aquel Entonces [In Years Gone By]: Readings in Mexican-American History* (Bloomington: Indiana University Press, 2000), 151.
12. Rose Cohen, "A Child Worker in the Garment Industry," in Paula S. Fass and Mary Ann Mason, eds., *Childhood in America* (New York: New York University Press, 2000), 259.
13. Quoted in Russell Freedman, *Immigrant Kids* (New York: Scholastic, 1980), 43–44.
14. Quoted in Judith E. Smith, *Family Connections: A History of Italian and Jewish Immigrant Lives in Providence, Rhode Island, 1900–1940* (Albany: SUNY Press, 1985), 54–56.
15. "Milwaukee's Newsboys' Republic," *The Outlook* 52 (April 5, 1913): 743–744, in CUAP 1/25/06.
16. Quoted in Richard A. Varbero, "Philadelphia's South Italians in the 1920s," in Allen F. Davis and Mark H. Haller, eds., *The Peoples of Philadelphia: A History of Ethnic Groups and Lower-Class Life, 1790–1940* (Philadelphia: Temple University Press, 1973), 256.
17. Quoted in Ronald Takaki, *Strangers from a Different Shore: A History of Asian Americans*, 2nd ed. (Boston: Little, Brown, 1998), 172–173.
18. United States Immigration Commission, *The Children of Immigrants in Schools* (Washington, D.C.: Government Printing Office, 1911).
19. Berrol, "School Days on the Old East Side," 201.
20. Jerre Mangione, *America Is Also Italian* (New York: G. P. Putnam's Sons, 1969), 50.
21. Kaufman and Knorr, "By Foot, by Horse, by Crummy," 50.

22. U.S. Immigration Commission, *The Children of Immigrants in Schools*, 51.
23. Maxine Seller, "The Education of Immigrant Children in Buffalo, New York, 1890–1916," *New York History* 57 (April 1976): 188.
24. Quoted in Berrol, "School Days on the Old East Side," 202.
25. A. R. Dugmore, "New Citizens for the Republic," 1903, in Moquin, *Makers of America: Natives and Aliens*, 275.
26. M. C. Darsie, "A Preliminary Report on the Mental Capacity of Japanese Children in California," in Paul B. Waterhouse, *The Future of Japanese-American Relations in California* (n.p., 1922), 25–26.
27. William A. Sheldon, "Educational Research and Statistics: The Intelligence of Mexican Children," 1924, in Lewis H. Carlson and George A. Colburn, *In Their Place: White America Defines Her Minorities, 1850–1950* (New York: John Wiley & Sons, 1972), 150–151.
28. "Mexico in San Antonio," in Wayne Moquin, ed., with Charles Van Doren, *A Documentary History of the Mexican Americans* (New York: Praeger, 1971), 262–263.
29. Randall C. Teeuwen, "Public Rural Education and the Americanization of the Germans from Russia in Colorado, 1900–1930," *Journal of the American Historical Society of Germans from Russia* 19 (Summer 1996): 12.
30. Bodnar, *The Transplanted*, 193.
31. "Graduation Day Has Become a Jewish Holiday," 1924, in Wayne Moquin, ed., *Makers of America: Hyphenated Americans, 1914–1924* (New York: Encyclopaedia Britannia Educational Corp., 1971), 270.
32. Thomas Čapek, *The Čzechs (Bohemians) in America: A Study of Their National, Cultural, Political, Social, Economic, and Religious Life* (Boston: Houghton Mifflin, 1920), 103.
33. "Kiddies Enjoy Treat: First Thanksgiving Is Observed by Youngsters at Laham Park Center," *Milwaukee Sentinel*, November 25, 1920, CUAP 1/25/06.
34. Quoted in Donna R. Gabaccia, *We Are What We Eat: Ethnic Food and the Making of Americans* (Cambridge: Harvard University Press, 1998), 55.
35. Jacob Riis, "Saluting the Flag," 1895, in Bremner, *Children and Youth in America*, Vol. II, *1866–1932*, 58.
36. Judith Raftery, "Progressivism Moves into the Schools: Los Angeles, 1905–1918," *California History* 66 (June 1987): 94.
37. Galarza, *Barrio Boy*, 207–212.
38. *Jewish Messenger*, September 25, 1891.
39. Galarza, *Barrio Boy*, 236–237.

40. Mary Tape, San Francisco, to Board of Education, San Francisco, April 8, 1885, in Andrew Carroll, ed., *Letters of a Nation: A Collection of Extraordinary American Letters* (New York: Broadway Books, 1997), 184–186.

41. Roger Daniels, *The Politics of Prejudice: The Anti-Japanese Movement in California and the Struggle for Japanese Exclusion* (Berkeley: University of California Press, 1962), 31–39.

42. Alfred Schultz quoted in Matthew Frye Jacobson, *Whiteness of a Different Color: European Immigrants and the Alchemy of Race* (Cambridge: Harvard University Press, 1998), 5.

43. Grove Johnson, "The Sexual Dangers of School Integration," 1909, in Carlson and Colburn, *In Their Place*, 232.

44. John Box, speech to the U.S. Congress, February 9, 1928, in S. T. Joshi, ed., *Documents of American Prejudice: An Anthology of Writings on Race from Thomas Jefferson to David Duke* (New York: Basic Books, 1999), 480.

45. Rodolfo Acuña, *Occupied America: A History of Chicanos*, 2nd ed. (New York: Harper & Row, 1981), 133.

46. "The United States Supreme Court Holds That Chinese Must Go to 'Colored Schools,'" 1927, in Carlson and Colburn, *In Their Place*, 196–197.

47. Quoted in Takaki, *Strangers from a Different Shore*, 182.

48. Mary Paik Lee's narrative, in Thomas Dublin, ed., *Immigrant Voices: New Lives in America, 1773–1986* (Urbana: University of Illinois Press, 1993), 180–181.

49. Richard and Ruth Dahl Chisholm, "Vignettes of a Prairie Childhood: Anecdotes of a Swedish-American Immigrant Life in North Dakota," *Swedish-American Historical Quarterly* 55 (April 2004): 97.

50. Bruno Lasker, *Race Attitudes in Children* (New York: Henry Holt, 1929), 4.

51. Ibid., 51.

52. John Foster Carr, "The Coming of the Italian," 1906, in Wayne Moquin with Charles Van Doren, eds., *A Documentary History of the Italian Americans* (New York: Praeger, 1974), 280.

53. Harry Roskolenko, "America, the Thief: A Jewish Search for Freedom," in Thomas C. Wheeler, ed., *The Immigrant Experience: The Anguish of Becoming American* (New York: Dial Press, 1971), 153.

54. E. N. Clopper, "Children on the Streets of Cincinnati," 1908, in Marten, *Childhood and Child Welfare in the Progressive Era*, 66–67.

55. Simon, *Bronx Primitive*, 50.

56. Priscilla Ferguson Clement, *Growing Pains: Children in the Industrial Age, 1850–1890* (New York: Twayne, 1997), 152.

57. Quoted in Takaki, *Strangers from a Different Shore*, 214.

58. Quoted in Garcia, "La Familia," in Barrera, Camarillo, and Hernandez, *Work, Family, Sex Roles, Language*, 131.

59. Richard Gambino, *Blood of My Blood: The Dilemma of the Italian-Americans* (Garden City: Doubleday, 1974), 230; Francis X. Femminella and Jill S. Quadagno, "The Italian American Family," in Charles H. Mindel and Robert Wittabenstein, *Ethnic Families in America: Patterns and Variations* (New York: Elsevier, 1976), 67.

60. Quoted in Constantine M. Panunzio, *The Soul of an Immigrant* (New York: Macmillan, 1934), 254, italics in original. It should be noted that Panunzio was quoting this woman with disapprobation; he believed that language schools were detrimental to the process of Americanization.

61. Quoted in Adele L. Younis, *The Coming of Arabic-Speaking People to the United States*, Philip M. Kayal, ed. (New York: Center for Migration Studies, 1995), 193–194.

62. Davorin Krmpotić to *Katolički Lit* [*The Catholic Newspaper*], September 24, 1925, quoted in Ivan Cizmić, "Letters of Croatian Priests from the United States to Croatia About the Life of Croatian Immigrants (1894–1940)," in Walter Hölbling and Reinhold Wagnleitner, eds., *The European Emigrant Experience in the U.S.A.* (Tübingen, Germany: Gunter Narr Verlag, 1992), 138.

63. Bishop John Baptist Scalabrini to Bishop Giuseppe Sarto, quoted in Silvano M. Tomas, ed., *For the Love of Immigrants: Migration Writings and Letters of Bishop John Baptist Scalabrini* (New York: Center for Migration Studies, 2000), 224.

64. Kevin Kenny, *The American Irish: A History* (New York: Longman, 2000), 167.

65. Jo Ellen McNergney Vinyard, *For Faith and Fortune: The Education of Catholic Immigrants in Detroit, 1805–1925* (Urbana: University of Illinois Press, 1998), 165.

66. Quoted in Edith Abbott and Sophonisba Breckinridge, *Truancy and Non-Attendance in the Chicago Schools: A Study of the Social Aspects of the Compulsory Education and Child Labor Legislation of Illinois* (Chicago: University of Chicago Press, 1917), 281–283.

67. A. G. Toth, "How We Should Live in America," quoted in Moquin, *Makers of America: Natives and Aliens*, 243.

68. "Appeal to Czech America," quoted in Moquin, *Makers of America: Hyphenated Americans*, 210.

69. "The Eleven National Commandments Aimed at Instilling a Modern National Consciousness," translated and reproduced in Subtelny, *Ukrainians in North America*, 110.

70. Harry Kitano and Roger Daniels, *Asian Americans: Emerging Minorities*, 3rd ed. (Upper Saddle River, N.J.: Prentice-Hall, 2001), 123; H. Brett Melendy, *Asians in America: Filipinos, Koreans, and East Indians* (Boston: Twayne, 1977), 143.

71. Iris Chang, *The Chinese in America: A Narrative History* (New York: Penguin, 2003), 182.

72. Pardee Lowe, *Father and Glorious Descendant* (Boston: Little, Brown, 1943), 108.

73. Jade Snow Wong's narrative in Wheeler, *The Anguish of Becoming American*, 115.

74. Stephen S. Fugita and David O'Brien, *Japanese American Ethnicity: The Persistence of Community* (Seattle: University of Washington Press, 1991), 88.

75. Harry Kitano, "A Hyphenated Identity," in Becky Thompson and Sangeeta Tyagi, eds., *Names We Call Home: Autobiography on Racial Identity* (New York: Routledge, 1996), 111.

76. Ronald Takaki, *Issei and Nissei: The Settling of Japanese America* (New York: Chelsea House, 1994).

77. Unsigned letter, San Francisco, January 21, 1893, in Hale, *Danes in North America*, 144–145.

78. Quoted in Harvey Green, *The Uncertainty of Everyday Life, 1914–1945* (New York: HarperCollins, 1992), 136.

79. "An Oral History of the Italians in Milwaukee," Part 2, CUAP 1/25/06.

80. Bruna Pieracci's narrative, in Salvatore J. LaGumina, ed., *The Immigrant Speaks: Italian Americans Tell Their Story* (New York: Center for Migration Studies, 1979), 39.

81. Quoted in Takaki, *Strangers from a Different Shore*, 224–225.

Chapter 4. Adolescent Years

1. Hilda Satt Polacheck, *I Came a Stranger: The Story of a Hull-House Girl*, ed. Dena J. Polacheck Epstein (Urbana: University of Illinois Press, 1989), 52.

2. Smith, *Family Connections*, 58.

3. Kathy Peiss, *Cheap Amusements: Working Women and Leisure in Turn-of-the-Century New York* (Philadelphia: Temple University Press, 1986), 72.

4. Sánchez, *Becoming Mexican-American*, 34.

5. John E. Bodnar, "Socialization and Adaptation," 159.

6. Huping Ling, "Family and Marriage of Late-Nineteenth and Early-Twentieth Century Chinese Immigrant Women," *Journal of American Ethnic History* 19 (Winter 2000): 45.

7. Søren Kjær quoted in Hale, *Danes in North America*, 151.

8. S. J. Kleinberg, "Children's and Mothers' Wage Labor in Three Eastern U.S. Cities, 1880–1920," *Social Science History* 29 (Spring 2005): 52–53.

9. Quoted in Bodnar, *The Transplanted*, 73.

10. George S. Counts, "The Selective Nature of American Secondary Education," 1922, in Bremner, *Children and Youth in America*, Vol. II: *1866–1932*, 1394.

11. Karel D. Bicha, "Hunkies: Stereotyping the Slavic Immigrants, 1890–1920," *Journal of American Ethnic History* 2 (Fall 1982): 28.

12. Richard A. Barbero, "Philadelphia's South Italians in the 1920s," in Davis and Haller, *The Peoples of Philadelphia*, 261–262.

13. Thomas C. Hunt, "Public Schools, 'Americanism,' and the Immigrant at the Turn of the Century," *Journal of General Education* 26 (Summer 1974): 151.

14. Dominick Cavallo, *Muscles and Morals: Organized Playgrounds and Urban Reform, 1880–1920* (Philadelphia: University of Pennsylvania Press, 1981).

15. Konrad Bercovici, *On New Shores* (New York: Century Co., 1925), 130.

16. Brunner, *Immigrant Farmers and Their Children*, 176.

17. Kitano and Daniels, *Asian Americans*, 90; quoted in Takaki, *Strangers from a Different Shore*, 57.

18. Leonard Dinnerstein, *Uneasy at Home: Antisemitism and the American Jewish Experience* (New York: Columbia University Press, 1987), 47–48.

19. Excerpt of John Foster Carr, "Guide to the United States for the Jewish Immigrant," reprinted in *Jewish Comment*, August 30, 1912.

20. "What America Means," 1916, in Moquin, *Makers of America: Hyphenated Americans*, 22.

21. Chauncey Depew, "Political Mission of the United States," 1888, in Joshi, *Documents of American Prejudice*, 506.

22. "The Raw Material" and "Two Years Later" in Thomas Burgess, *Foreign-Born Americans and Their Children: Our Duty and Opportunity for God and Country from the Standpoint of the Episcopal Church* (New York: Department of Missions and Church Extensions of the Episcopal Church, 1921), 34.

23. Chisholm, "Vignettes of a Prairie Childhood," 84, 99.

24. Sara R. O'Brien, *English for Foreigners*, 1909, quoted in David B. Tyack, ed., *Turning Points in American Educational History* (Lexington, Mass.: Xerox College Publishing, 1967), 240.

25. Dugmore, "New Citizens for the Republic," in Moquin, *Makers of America: Natives and Aliens,* 274. David Nasaw's study *Children of the City: At Work and at Play* (Garden City, N.Y.: Anchor/Doubleday, 1985) reinforces this point about the shared political interests of immigrant boys at school and on the streets.

26. Quoted in Chang, *The Chinese in America*, 195.

27. Yoshiko Uchida quoted in Paul R. Spickard, *Japanese Americans: The Formation and Transformation of an Ethnic Group* (New York: Twayne, 1996), 80.

28. M. E. Ravage, *An American in the Making: The Life Story of an Immigrant* (reprint, New York: Dover, 1971), 76–78.

29. Waclaw Kruszka, *A History of the Poles in America to 1908, Part I*, ed. James S. Pula, trans. Krystyna Jankowski (Washington, D.C.: Catholic University of America Press, 1993), 20.

30. Quoted in Myron B. Kuropas, *The Ukrainian Americans: Roots and Aspirations, 1884–1954* (Toronto: University of Toronto Press, 1991), 94.

31. Czech-American Central School Association, "Appeal to Czech America," 1918, in Moquin, *Makers of America: Hyphenated Americans,* 210–211.

32. Editorial, December 7, 1912, *Hawaii Hochi*, in Franklin Odo, ed., *The Columbia Documentary History of the Asian American Experience* (New York: Columbia University Press, 2002), 158.

33. George G. Bruntz, "German-Russians," transcript of lecture given to the Adams County, Nebraska, Historical Society, July 28, 1974, Adams County Historical Society Papers, Folder 1, MSS 029, Historical Society of Pennsylvania.

34. Flora Belle Jan quoted in Takaki, *Strangers from a Different Shore*, 258.

35. "How a Girl Can Be Most Helpful at Home," *S.E.G. News*, April 8, 1916, in bound volume of *S.E.G. News* issues, 1914–1917, American Jewish Historical Society.

36. Joan Morrison and Charlotte Fox Zabusky, eds., *American Mosaic: The Immigrant Experience in the Words of Those Who Lived It* (Pittsburgh: University of Pittsburgh Press, 1993), 68.

37. Jane Addams, "Italian Immigrant Children in Chicago," 1902, in Bremner, *Children and Youth in America*, Vol. II: *1866–1932*, 1323.

38. Emily Greene Balch, *Our Slavic Fellow Citizens* (New York: Charities Publication Committee, 1910), 415.

39. Robert A. Orsi, "The Fault of Memory: 'Southern Italy' in the Imagination of Immigrants and the Lives of Their Children in Italian Harlem, 1920–1945," *Journal of Family History* 15 (1990): 135–136.

40. Jane Addams, "Generation Conflicts Among the Immigrants," 1910, in Moquin, *Makers of America: The New Immigrants, 1904–1913* (New York: Encyclopaedia Britannica Educational Corp., 1971), 243–244.

41. Jane Addams, "Generation Conflicts Among the Immigrants," 1910, in Moquin, *Makers of America: The New Immigrants*, 245.

42. William I. Thomas and Florian Znaniecki, "Juvenile Delinquency Among Polish-American Children in Chicago, 1918," in Bremner, *Children and Youth in America*, Vol. II: *1866–1932*, 594–597.

43. Lillie Leung quoted in Chang, *The Chinese in America*, 180.

44. Mrs. E. M. Findlay quoted in Takaki, *Strangers from a Different Shore*, 258.

45. Sánchez, *Becoming Mexican-American*, 141.

46. Toth, "How We Should Live in America," in Moquin, *Makers of America: Natives and Aliens*, 243.

47. Vicki L. Ruiz, *From Out of the Shadows: Mexican Women in Twentieth-Century America* (New York: Oxford University Press, 1998), 59.

48. Kruszka, *A History of the Poles in America to 1908*, Part I, 247.

49. Leonard Covello's autobiographical notes, Box 20, Folder 17, Leonard Covello Papers, MSS Group 40, Historical Society of Pennsylvania.

50. Adolph B. Beson and Naboth Hedin, eds., *Swedes in America, 1638–1938* (New Haven: Yale University Press, 1938), 69.

51. Yukari Takai, "Shared Earnings, Unequal Responsibilities: Single French-Canadian Wage-Earning Women in Lowell, Massachusetts, 1900–1920," *Labour/Le Travail* 47 (Spring 2001): 21.

52. Lillie Leung quoted in Takaki, *Strangers from a Different Shore*, 259.

53. Dinnerstein, *Uneasy at Home*, 48.

54. María Bjerg, "A Tale of Two Settlements: Danish Immigrants on the American Prairie and the Argentine Pampa, 1860–1930," *Annals of Iowa* 59 (Winter 2000): 7.

55. "A Happy Boy," Dakota Territory, January 1888, in Hale, *Danes in North America*, 47.

56. Clara Corica Grillo's narrative in LaGumina, *The Immigrants Speak*, 116.

A Note on Sources

IN ORDER TO write *Small Strangers* I looked into a wide variety of primary and secondary sources. The topic of immigrant children lies at the intersection of numerous fields of American history, including immigration, family structure, social welfare and reform, education, health care, prejudice and discrimination, and specific ethnic groups. Historians in all these fields have often included children in their work without necessarily focusing on them. Historians of childhood and youth by definition put children at center stage, and many have paid attention to the differences that racial, gender, religious, and ethnic backgrounds make on their lives. But there has been almost no sustained attention to immigrant children as a group. So here I have chosen to highlight the sources I found most useful in piecing together a history of late-nineteenth- and early-twentieth-century immigrant children in America. Whenever possible I have included both classic works and new scholarship. I have also highlighted the most accessible published primary sources rather than the manuscript collections from various archives that I also consulted. The entries are presented in alphabetical order within each paragraph.

Primary Sources

A number of documentary collections are concerned with immigration and childhood and offer a useful starting point for the history of immigrant children. On childhood and youth in America, see Robert H. Bremner, ed., *Children and Youth in America: A Documentary History*, Volume

II: *1886–1932* (Cambridge: Harvard University Press, 1971); Paula S. Fass and Mary Ann Mason, eds., *Childhood in America* (New York: New York University Press, 2000); and James Marten, ed., *Childhood and Child Welfare in the Progressive Era: A Brief History with Documents* (Boston: Bedford/St. Martin's, 2005).

General documentary collections on immigration, which offer many kinds of individual, family, and communal accounts, include Ann Banks, ed., *First-Person America* (New York: Knopf, 1980); Frank J. Coppa and Thomas J. Curran, eds., *The Immigrant Experience in America* (Boston: Twayne, 1976); Thomas Dublin, ed., *Immigrant Voices: New Lives in America, 1773–1986* (Urbana: University of Illinois Press, 1993); Hamilton Holt, ed., *The Life Stories of Undistinguished Americans as Told by Themselves,* 2nd ed. (New York: Routledge, 1990); Gordon Hutner, ed., *Immigrant Voices: Twenty-Four Narratives on Becoming American* (New York: Signet, 1999); Wayne Moquin, ed., *Makers of America: Hyphenated Americans, 1914–1924; Natives and Aliens, 1891–1903; The New Immigrants, 1904–1913* (Encyclopaedia Britannica Educational Corp., 1971); Joan Morrison and Charlotte Fox Zabusky, eds., *American Mosaic: The Immigrant Experience in the Words of Those Who Lived It* (Pittsburgh: University of Pittsburgh Press, 1993); June Namias, ed., *First Generation: In the Words of Twentieth-Century American Immigrants* (Boston: Beacon Press, 1978); and Thomas C. Wheeler, ed., *The Immigrant Experience: The Anguish of Becoming American* (New York: Dial Press, 1971).

More specialized documentary collections offer in-depth looks at particular groups. See, for example, H. Arnold Barton, ed., *Letters from the Promised Land: Swedes in America, 1840–1914* (Minneapolis: University of Minnesota Press, 1975); Frank Chin, ed., *Born in the U.S.A.: A Story of Japanese America, 1889–1947* (Lanham, Md.: Rowman & Littlefield, 2002); Frederick Hale, ed., *Danes in North America* (Seattle: University of Washington Press, 1984); Salvatore J. LaGumina, ed., *The Immigrants Speak: Italian Americans Tell Their Story* (New York: Center for Migration Studies, 1979); Jacob Rader Marcus, ed., *The Jew in the American World: A Source Book* (Detroit: Wayne State University Press, 1996); Steven Mintz, ed., *Mexican American Voices* (St. James, N.Y.: Brandywine Press, 2000); Wayne Moquin with Charles Van Doren, eds., *A Documentary History of the Italian Americans* (New York: Praeger, 1974); Wayne Moquin with Charles Van Doren, *A Documentary History of the Mexican Americans* (New York: Praeger, 1971); Franklin Odo, ed., *The Columbia Documentary History of the Asian American Experience* (New York: Columbia University Press, 2002); and Judy Yung, Gordon H. Chang, and Him Mark Lai, eds., *Chinese American Voices: From the Gold Rush to the Present* (Berkeley: University of California Press, 2006).

Memoirs and autobiographies are among the liveliest sources for the history of immigrant children. A small sample of rewarding examples of this genre includes Peter T. Campon, *The Evolution of an Immigrant* (Brooklyn: Theo. Gaus, 1960); Pascal D'Angelo, *Son of Italy* (New York: Macmillan, 1924); Marie Hall Ets, *Rosa: The Life of an Italian Immigrant*, 2nd ed. (Madison: University of Wisconsin Press, 1999); Ernesto Galarza, *Barrio Boy* (Notre Dame: University of Notre Dame Press, 1971); Maurice Hindus, *Green Worlds: An Informal Chronicle* (New York: Doubleday, Doran & Co., 1938); Bill Hosokawa, *Out of the Frying Pan: Reflections of a Japanese American* (Niwot, Colo.: University Press of Colorado, 1998); Carl Christian Jensen, *An American Saga* (Boston: Little, Brown, 1927); Pardee Lowe, *Father and Glorious Descendant* (Boston: Little, Brown, 1943); Constantine M. Panunzio, *The Soul of an Immigrant* (New York: Macmillan, 1934); Angelo Pellegrini, *Immigrant's Return* (New York: Macmillan, 1951); M. E. Ravage, *An American in the Making: The Life Story of an Immigrant* (New York: Dover Publications, 1971); Nils Nelson Rønning, *Fifty Years in America* (Minneapolis: Fried Publishing Co., 1938); Kate Simon, *Bronx Primitive: Portraits in a Childhood* (New York: Penguin, 1982); Adrienne Thompson, *The Octagonal Heart* (Indianapolis: Bobbs-Merrill, 1956); and Peter Yankoff, *Peter Menikoff: The Story of a Bulgarian Boy in the Great American Melting Pot* (Nashville: Cokesbury Press, 1928).

At the turn of the last century, as at the turn of the present century, immigration was a hotly contested part of the national discourse. Americans from all walks of life weighed in on the broad civic discussion of immigration. Contemporary contributions to this debate include Emily Greene Balch, *Our Slavic Fellow Citizens* (New York: Charities Publication Committee, 1910); Konrad Bercovici, *On New Shores* (New York: Century

Co., 1925); and T. J. Woofter, Jr., *Race and Ethnic Groups in American Life* (New York: McGraw-Hill, 1933).

Other contemporary accounts focused on specific ethnic groups. The authors of these studies ranged from those highly sympathetic to immigrants to those whose goal was to encourage immigration restriction. See Emory S. Bogardus, *The Mexican in the United States* (Los Angeles: University of Southern California Press, 1934); Thomas Burgess, *Greeks in America: An Account of Their Coming, Progress, Customs, Living, and Aspirations* (Boston: Sherman, French & Co., 1913); Thomas Čapek, *The Čzechs (Bohemians) in America: A Study of Their National, Cultural, Political, Social, Economic, and Religious Life* (Boston: Houghton Mifflin, 1920); Elmer T. Clark, *The Latin Immigrant in the South* (Nashville: Cokesbury Press, 1924); Sidney L. Gulick, *The American Japanese Problem: A Study of Race Relations of the East and the West* (New York: Charles Scribner's Sons, 1914); Alma A. Guttersen and Regina Hilleboe Christensen, eds., *Norse-American Women, 1825–1925* (Minneapolis: Lutheran Free Church Publishing, 1926); Yamato Ichikashi, *Japanese in the United States: A Critical Study of the Problems of the Japanese Immigrants and Their Children* (Stanford: Stanford University Press, 1932); and J. P. Xenides, *The Greeks in America* (New York: George H. Doran, 1922).

A considerable part of this literature made special reference to immigrant children, recognized by many as the faces of a potentially new America in future generations. Some examples include Bertha M. Boody, *A Psychological Study of Immigrant Children at Ellis Island* (Baltimore: Williams & Wilkins, 1926); Edmund DeS. Brunner, *Immigrant Farmers and Their Children* (Garden City, N.Y.: Doubleday, Doran & Co., 1929); Niles Carpenter, *Immigrants and Their Children, 1920* (Washington, D.C.: Government Printing Office, 1927); John C. Gebhart, *The Growth and Development of Italian Children in New York City* (New York: New York Association for Improving the Condition of the Poor, 1924); and United States Immigration Commission, *The Children of Immigrants in Schools*, Volume I (Washington, D.C.: Government Printing Office, 1911). Psychologist Bruno Lasker investigated children's attitudes toward children of different backgrounds in *Race Attitudes in Children* (New York: Henry Holt, 1929).

Another important category of primary sources for this book is the large body of material produced by progressive reformers and social welfare advocates during the late 1800s and early 1900s. The emergence of the social sciences contemporaneously with mass immigration provided ample opportunity for social research. Some studies approached immigration in general, such as Edith Abbott, ed., *Immigration: Select Documents and Case Records* (New York: Arno Press, 1969); Edith Abbott, *The Tenements of Chicago, 1908–1935* (Chicago: University of Chicago Press, 1936); and Paul Edward Kellogg, ed., *Wage-Earning Pittsburgh* (New York: Survey Associates, 1914). Others focused on issues most relevant to children. Examples include Edith Abbott and Sophonisba Breckinridge, *Truancy and Non-Attendance in the Chicago Schools: A Study of the Social Aspects of the Compulsory Education and Child Labor Legislation of Illinois* (Chicago: University of Chicago Press, 1917); Child-Study Society Section of the Wisconsin Teachers' Association, *Handbook of the Wisconsin Child-Study Society* (Milwaukee: Wisconsin Child-Study Society, 1898); Mary McHenry Cox, *Advantages of Institutions in the Education of Immigrant Children* (Philadelphia: n.p., 1887); Alex Hrdlicka, *Anthropological Investigations on One Thousand White and Colored Children of Both Sexes of the Inmates of the New York Juvenile Asylum* (New York: Wynhoop Hallenbeck Crawford Co., 1898); New Century Club of Philadelphia, comp., *Statutes of Every State in the United States Concerning Dependent, Neglected, and Delinquent Children* (Philadelphia: George F. Lasher, 1900); and Pennsylvania Child Labor Committee, *The Working Child and the Law* (n.p., 1906). All these studies, whether carried out by social service professionals or lay reformers, operated under the progressive assumption that the best way to effect reform was first to identify the problem, then offer a solution.

Secondary Sources

When beginning to develop the field, historians of childhood and youth published a significant amount of their work in anthology format. See collections such as Joe Austin and Michael Nevin Willard, eds., *Generations of Youth: Youth Cultures and History in Twentieth-Century America*

(New York: New York University Press, 1998); Glenn H. Elder, Jr., John Modell, and Ross Parke, eds., *Children in Time and Place: Developmental and Historical Insights* (New York: Cambridge University Press, 1993); Harvey J. Graff, ed., *Growing Up in America: Historical Experiences* (Detroit: Wayne State University Press, 1987); N. Ray Hiner and Joseph Hawes, *Growing Up in America: Children in Historical Perspective* (Urbana: University of Illinois Press, 1985); Sherrie A. Inness, ed., *Delinquents and Debutantes: Twentieth-Century American Girls' Cultures* (New York: New York University Press, 1998); and Elliott West and Paula Petrik, eds., *Small Worlds: Children and Adolescents in America, 1850–1950* (Lawrence: University Press of Kansas, 1992).

Other important works on the history of childhood and youth include Selma Cantor Berrol, *Growing Up American: Immigrant Children in America Then and Now* (New York: Twayne, 1995); Joan Jacobs Brumberg, *The Body Project: An Intimate History of American Girls* (New York: Random House, 1997); Priscilla Ferguson Clement, *Growing Pains: Children in the Industrial Age, 1850–1890* (New York: Twayne, 1997); Gary S. Cross, *Kids' Stuff: Toys and the Changing World of American Childhood* (Cambridge: Harvard University Press, 1997); John Demos, *Past, Present, and Personal: The Family and Life Course in American History* (New York: Oxford University Press, 1986); Paula S. Fass, *The Damned and the Beautiful: American Youth in the 1920s* (New York: Oxford University Press, 1977); Harvey J. Graff, *Conflicting Paths: Growing Up in America* (Cambridge: Harvard University Press, 1995); Thomas Hine, *The Rise and Fall of the American Teenager* (New York: Avon Books, 1999); Marilyn Irvin Holt, *Children of the Western Plains: The Nineteenth-Century Experience* (Chicago: Ivan R. Dee, 2003); Jane H. Hunter, *How Young Ladies Became Girls: The Victorian Origins of American Girlhood* (New Haven: Yale University Press, 2003); Joseph F. Kett, *Rites of Passage: Adolescence in America, 1790 to the Present* (New York: Basic Books, 1977); Kriste Lindenmeyer, *The Greatest Generation Grows Up: American Childhood in the 1930s* (Chicago: Ivan R. Dee, 2005); David Nasaw, *Children of the City: At Work and at Play* (New York: Oxford University Press, 1985); Grace Palladino, *Teenagers: An American History* (New York: Basic Books, 1996); Elliott

West, *Growing Up in Twentieth-Century America: A History and Reference Guide* (Westport, Conn.: Greenwood Press, 1996); and Viviana Zelizer, *Pricing the Priceless Child: The Changing Social Value of Children* (New York: Basic Books, 1985). Two recent single-volume works on the history of American childhood are Joseph E. Illick, *American Childhoods* (Philadelphia: University of Pennsylvania Press, 2002), and Steven Mintz, *Huck's Raft: A History of American Childhood* (New York: Belknap, 2004).

Identifying major secondary sources on American immigration and ethnic history is an immense task, given the scope of the literature. Essential reading includes (but is certainly not limited to) Elliott Robert Barkan, ed., *A Nation of Peoples: A Sourcebook in America's Multicultural Heritage* (Westport, Conn.: Greenwood Press, 1999); John E. Bodnar, *The Transplanted: A History of Immigrants in Urban America* (Bloomington, Ind.: Indiana University Press, 1985); Roger Daniels, *Coming to America: A History of Immigration and Ethnicity in American Life* (New York: HarperCollins, 1990); Leonard Dinnerstein, Roger L. Nichols, and David M. Reimers, *Natives and Strangers: A Multicultural History of Americans* (New York: Oxford University Press, 1996); Lawrence H. Fuchs, *The American Kaleidoscope: Race, Ethnicity, and the Civic Culture* (Hanover, N.H.: Wesleyan University Press, 1990); Donna R. Gabaccia, *From the Other Side: Women, Gender, and Immigrant Life in the United States, 1820–1990* (Bloomington: Indiana University Press, 1994); Oscar Handlin, *The Uprooted*, 2nd ed. (Philadelphia: University of Pennsylvania Press, 2000); Matthew Frye Jacobson, *Whiteness of a Different Color: European Immigrants and the Alchemy of Race* (Cambridge: Harvard University Press, 1998); and Doris Weatherford, *Foreign and Female: Immigrant Women in America, 1840–1930* (New York: Facts on File, 1995).

For further reading on Americanization, see James Barrett, "Americanization from the Bottom Up: Immigration and the Remaking of the Working Class in the United States, 1880–1930," *Journal of American History* 79 (December 1992): 996–1020; Robert A. Carlson, *The Quest for Conformity: Americanization Through Education* (New York: John Wiley, 1975); Timothy J. Hatton, "The Immigrant Assimilation Problem in Late Nineteenth-Century America," *Journal of Economic History* 57 (March

1997): 34–62; and John F. McClymer, "Gender and the 'American Way of Life': Women in the Americanization Movement," *Journal of American Ethnic History* 10 (Spring 1991): 3–20.

Prejudice and discrimination have always accompanied every facet of American immigration. These issues are explored in Lewis H. Carlson and George A. Colburn, *In Her Place: White America Defines Her Minorities, 1850–1950* (New York: John Wiley, 1972); Roger Daniels, *Guarding the Golden Door: American Immigration Policy and Immigrants Since 1882* (New York: Hill & Wang, 2004); Mae M. Ngai, *Impossible Subjects: Illegal Aliens and the Making of Modern America* (Princeton: Princeton University Press, 2003); and Benjamin B. Ringer, *We the People and Others: Duality and America's Treatment of Its Racial Minorities* (New York: Tavistock Publications, 1983).

Social history in general and the fields of family history and women's history in particular often intersect with immigration history. Representative works include Karen Anderson, *Changing Women: A History of Racial Ethnic Women in Modern America* (New York: Oxford University Press, 1996); John E. Bodnar, "Immigration, Kinship, and the Rise of Working Class Realism in Industrial America," *Journal of Social History* 14 (Fall 1980): 45–66; George J. Borjas, "Long-Run Convergence of Ethnic Skill Differentials: The Children and Grandchildren of the Great Migration," *Industrial and Labor Relations Review* 47 (July 1994): 553–573; Sheri Broder, "Informing the 'Cruelty': The Monitoring of Respectability in Philadelphia's Working Class Neighborhoods in the Late Nineteenth Century," *Radical America* 21 (Summer 1987): 34–47; Hasia R. Diner, *Hungering for America: Italian, Irish, and Jewish Foodways in the Age of Migration* (Cambridge: Harvard University Press, 2001); Donna R. Gabaccia, *We Are What We Eat: Ethnic Food and the Making of Americans* (Cambridge: Harvard University Press, 1998); Linda Gordon, "Family Violence, Feminism, and Social Control," *Feminist Studies* 12 (Fall 1986): 453–478; Katrina Irving, *Immigrant Mothers: Narratives of Race and Maternity, 1890–1925* (Urbana: University of Illinois Press, 2000); S. J. Kleinberg, "Children's and Mothers' Wage Labor in Three Eastern U.S. Cities, 1880–1920," *Social Science History* 29 (Spring 2005): 45–76; Joanne

Meyerowitz, *Women Adrift: Independent Wage-Earners in Chicago, 1880–1930* (Chicago: University of Chicago Press, 1988); Charles H. Mindell and Robert Wittabenstein, *Ethnic Families in America: Patterns and Variations* (New York: Elsevier, 1976); Kathy Peiss, *Cheap Amusements: Working Women and Leisure in Turn-of-the-Century New York* (Philadelphia: Temple University Press, 1986); Elizabeth H. Pleck, *Celebrating the Family: Ethnicity, Consumer Culture, and Family Rituals* (Cambridge: Harvard University Press, 2000); Sharon Sassler, "Feathering the Nest or Flying the Coop? Ethnic and Gender Differences in Young Adults' Co-residence in 1910," *Journal of Family History* 21 (October 1996): 446–466; Sharon Sassler and Michael J. White, "Ethnicity, Gender, and Social Mobility in 1910," *Social Science History* 21 (Fall 1997): 321–357; and Jordan Stanger-Ross, Christina Collins, and Mark J. Stern, "Falling Far from the Tree: Transitions to Adulthood and the Social History of Twentieth-Century America," *Social Science History* 29 (2005): 625–648.

One of the major subjects embedded in the history of immigrant children is education. See Moses Isaiah Berger, *The Settlement, the Immigrant, and the Public School: A Study of the Influence of the Settlement Movement and the New Migration upon Public Education, 1890–1940* (New York: Arno Press, 1980 [original edition 1956]); Stephen F. Brumberg, *Going to America, Going to School: The Jewish Immigrant Public School Encounter in Turn-of-the-Century America* (New York: Praeger Press, 1986); Miriam Cohen, "Changing Education Strategies Among Immigrant Generations: New York Italians in Comparative Perspective," *Journal of Social History* 15 (Spring 1982): 443–466; Ronald D. Cohen, *Children of the Mill: Schooling and Society in Gary, Indiana, 1906–1960* (Bloomington: Indiana University Press, 1990); Lawrence Cremin, *American Education: The Metropolitan Experience, 1876–1980* (New York: Harper & Row, 1988); Paula S. Fass, *Outside In: Minorities and the Transformation of American Education* (New York: Oxford University Press, 1989); Claudia Goldin, "America's Graduation from High School: The Evolution and Spread of Secondary Schooling in the Twentieth Century," *Journal of Economic History* 58 (June 1998): 345–374; Harvey Kantor and David B. Tyack, eds., *Work, Youth, and Schooling: Historical Perspectives on Vocationalism in American Education*

(Stanford: Stanford University Press, 1982); Jo Ellen McNergney Vinyard, *Faith and Fortune: The Education of Catholic Immigrants in Detroit, 1805–1925* (Urbana: University of Illinois Press, 1998); Joel Perlmann, *Ethnic Differences: Schooling and Social Structure Among the Irish, Italians, Jews, and Blacks in an American City, 1800–1935* (Cambridge: Cambridge University Press, 1988); Judith Raftery, "Progressivism Moves into the Schools: Los Angeles, 1905–1918," *California History* 66 (June 1987): 94–103; William J. Reese, *America's Public Schools: From the Common School to "No Child Left Behind"* (Baltimore: Johns Hopkins University Press, 2005); Maxine Seller, "The Education of Immigrant Children in Buffalo, New York, 1890–1916," *New York History* 57 (April 1976): 183–199; Timothy L. Smith, "Immigrant Social Aspirations and American Education, 1880–1930," *American Quarterly* 21 (Autumn 1969): 523–543; David B. Tyack, *The One Best System: A History of American Urban Education* (Cambridge: Harvard University Press, 1974); Reed Ueda, *Avenues to Adulthood: The Origins of the High School and Social Mobility in an American Suburb* (Cambridge: Cambridge University Press, 1997); and Bernard J. Weiss, ed., *American Education and the European Immigrant, 1840–1940* (Urbana: University of Illinois Press, 1982).

Progressive reformers of all kinds expended enormous amounts of time and energy on the problems of immigrants and immigration. Relevant works include Mina Carson, *Settlement Folk: The Evolution of Social Welfare Ideology in the American Settlement Movement, 1883–1930* (Chicago: University of Chicago Press, 1990); Dominick Cavallo, *Muscles and Morals: Organized Playgrounds and Urban Reform, 1880–1920* (Philadelphia: University of Pennsylvania Press, 1981); Elizabeth J. Clapp, *Mothers of All Children: Women Reformers and the Rise of Juvenile Courts in Progressive Era America* (University Park, Pa.: Penn State University Press, 1998); Cynthia A. Connolly, "Nurses: The Early Twentieth Century Tuberculosis Preventorium's 'Connecting Link,'" *Nursing History Review* 10 (2002): 127–157; Richard A. Meckel, *Save the Babies: American Public Health Reform and the Prevention of Infant Mortality, 1850–1929* (Baltimore: Johns Hopkins University Press, 1990); Mary E. Odem, *Delinquent Daughters: Protecting and Policing Adolescent Female Sexuality in the United States, 1885–1920* (Chapel Hill: University of North Carolina Press, 1995); David

S. Tanenhaus, "Between Dependency and Liberty: The Conundrum of Children's Rights in the Gilded Age," *Law and History Review* 23 (Summer 2005): 351–385; and Nurith Zmora, *Orphanages Reconsidered: Child Care Institutions in Progressive Era Baltimore* (Philadelphia: Temple University Press, 1994).

Some immigrant groups have attracted considerably more scholarly attention than others. Italians have enjoyed a much larger body of literature than Greeks, for example. Like the rest of the selected bibliography, the following suggestions for further reading are in no way meant to be comprehensive.

On central and western European immigrants, see Edward G. Hartmann, *Americans from Wales* (Boston: Christopher Publishing, 1967); Günter Mottman, ed., *Germans to America: Three Hundred Years of Immigration, 1683–1983* (Stuttgart: Institute for Foreign Cultural Relations, 1982); Richard O'Connor, *The German-Americans: An Informal History* (Boston: Little, Brown, 1968); E. Wilder Spaulding, *The Quiet Invaders: The Story of the Austrian Impact upon America* (Vienna: Österreichischer Bundersverlag, 1968); and Robert P. Swierenga, *Faith and Family: Dutch Immigration and Settlement in the United States, 1820–1920* (New York: Holmes & Meier, 2000).

On Chinese immigrants, see Iris Chang, *The Chinese in America: A Narrative History* (New York: Penguin, 2003); Huping Ling, "Family and Marriage of Late-Nineteenth and Early Twentieth-Century Chinese Immigrant Women," *Journal of American Ethnic History* (Winter 2000): 43–63; Haiming Liu, "The Trans-Pacific Family: A Case Study of Sam Chang's Family History," *Amerasia Journal* 18 (1992): 1–34; Ronald Takaki, *Strangers from a Different Shore: A History of Asian Americans*, 2nd ed. (Boston: Little, Brown, 1998); Shih-Shan Henry Tsai, *The Chinese Experience in America* (Bloomington: Indiana University Press, 1986); Judy Yung, *Chinese Women of America: A Pictorial History* (Seattle: University of Washington Press, 1986); and Liping Zhu, *A Chinaman's Chance: The Chinese on the Rocky Mountain Mining Frontier* (Nimot, Colo.: University Press of Colorado, 1997).

On French-Canadian immigrants, see Gerard J. Brault, *The French-Canadian Heritage in New England* (Hanover, N.H.: University Press of

New England, 1986), and Yukari Takai, "Shared Earnings, Unequal Responsibilities: Single French-Canadian Wage-Earning Women in Lowell, Massachusetts, 1900–1920," *Labour/Le Travail* 47 (Spring 2001): 1–29.

On Irish immigrants, see Dennis Clark, *Hibernia America: The Irish and Regional Cultures* (New York: Greenwood Press, 1986); Maureen Dezell, *Irish America Coming into Clover: The Evolution of a People and a Culture* (New York: Doubleday, 2000); Hasia R. Diner, *Erin's Daughters in America: Irish Immigrant Women in the Nineteenth Century* (Baltimore: Johns Hopkins University Press, 1983); Patricia Kelleher, "Maternal Strategies: Irish Women's Headship of Families in Gilded Age Chicago," *Journal of Women's History* 13 (2001): 80–106; Lawrence McCaffery, *Textures of Irish America* (Syracuse: Syracuse University Press, 1992); and Carl Wittke, *The Irish in America* (Baton Rouge: Louisiana State University Press, 1956).

On Italian immigrants, see Simone Cinotto, "Leonard Covello, the Covello Papers, and the History of Eating Habits Among Italian Immigrants in New York," *Journal of American History* 91 (September 2004): 497–521; Richard Gambino, *Blood of My Blood: The Dilemma of the Italian-Americans* (Garden City, N.Y.: Doubleday, 1974); Thomas A. Guglielmo, *White on Arrival: Italians, Race, Color, and Power in Chicago, 1890–1945* (New York: Oxford University Press, 2003); Michael La Sorte, *La Merica: Images of Italian Greenhorn Experiences* (Philadelphia: Temple University Press, 1985); Stefano Luconi, *From Paesani to White Ethnics: The Italian Experience in Philadelphia* (Albany, N.Y.: SUNY Press, 2001); Jerre Mangione and Ben Morreale, *La Storia: Five Centuries of the Italian-American Experience* (New York: HarperCollins, 1992); Anna Maria Martellone, "Italian Mass Emigration to the United States, 1876–1930: A Historical Survey," *Perspectives in American History*, New Series 1 (1984): 379–423; David A. J. Richards, *Italian Americans: The Racializing of an Ethnic Identity* (New York: New York University Press, 1999); Andrew F. Rolle, *The Italian-Americans: Troubled Roots* (New York: Free Press, 1980); and Allon Schoener, *The Italian Americans* (New York: Macmillan, 1987).

On Japanese immigrants, see Roger Daniels, *The Politics of Prejudice: The Anti-Japanese Movement in California and the Struggle for Japanese Exclusion* (Berkeley: University of California Press, 1962); Nancy Brown Diggs, *Steel Butterflies: Japanese Women and the American Experience* (Albany, N.Y.: SUNY Press, 1998); Stephen S. Fugita and David J. O'Brien, *Japanese American Ethnicity: The Persistence of Community* (Seattle: University of Washington Press, 1991); Bill Hosokawa, *Nisei: The Quiet Americans* (New York: William Morrow and Company, 1969); Yuji Ichioka, *The Issei: The World of First-Generation Japanese Immigrants, 1885–1924* (New York: Free Press, 1988); Yukiko Kimura, *Issei: Japanese Immigrants in Hawaii* (Honolulu: University of Hawaii Press, 1988); Gene N. Levine and Colbert Rhodes, *The Japanese-American Community: A Three-Generation Story* (New York: Praeger, 1981); John Modell, *The Economics and Politics of Racial Accommodation: The Japanese of Los Angeles, 1900–1942* (Urbana: University of Illinois Press, 1977); Mei T. Nakano, *Japanese American Women: Three Generations, 1890–1990* (Berkeley and San Francisco: Mina Press and National Japanese American Historical Society, 1990); David J. O'Brien and Stephen S. Fugita, *The Japanese American Experience* (Bloomington: Indiana University Press, 1991); Paul R. Spickard, *Japanese Americans: The Formation and Transformation of an Ethnic Group* (New York: Twayne, 1996); and Ronald Takaki, *Strangers from a Different Shore: A History of Asian Americans*, 2nd ed. (Boston: Little, Brown, 1998).

On Jewish immigrants, see Neil M. Cowan and Ruth Schwartz Cowan, *Our Parents' Lives: The Americanization of Eastern European Jews* (New York: Basic Books, 1989); Leonard Dinnerstein, *Uneasy at Home: Antisemitism and the American Jewish Experience* (New York: Columbia University Press, 1987); Ellen Eisenberg, *Jewish Agricultural Colonies in New Jersey, 1882–1920* (Syracuse: Syracuse University Press, 1995); Murray Friedman, ed., *Jewish Life in Philadelphia, 1840–1930* (Philadelphia: ISHI Publications, 1983); Reena Sigman Friedman, *These Are Our Children: Jewish Orphanages in the United States, 1880–1925* (Hanover, N.H.: Brandeis University Press, 1994); Arthur A. Goren, *New York's Jews and the Quest for Community: The Kehillah Experiment, 1908–1922* (New York: Columbia University Press, 1980); Andrew R. Heinze, *Adapting to Abundance: Jewish Immigrants, Mass Consumption, and the Search for American Identity* (New York: Columbia University Press, 1990); Irving Howe, *World of Our Fathers* (New York: Harcourt Brace Jovanovich, 1976); Melissa R. Klapper, *Jewish Girls Coming of Age in America, 1860–1920*

(New York University Press, 2005); Deborah Dash Moore, *At Home in America: Second Generation Jews in New York* (New York: Columbia University Press, 1981); Jonathan D. Sarna, *American Judaism: A History* (New Haven: Yale University Press, 2004); Gerald Sorin, *A Time for Building: The Third Migration, 1880–1920* (Baltimore: Johns Hopkins University Press, 1992); Gerald Sorin, *Tradition Transformed: The Jewish Experience in America* (Baltimore: Johns Hopkins University Press, 1997); Sydney Stahl Weinberg, *The World of Our Mothers: The Lives of Jewish Immigrant Women* (Chapel Hill: University of North Carolina Press, 1988); and Lee Shai Weissbach, *Jewish Life in Small-Town America: A History* (New Haven: Yale University Press, 2005).

On Mexican immigrants, see Rodolfo Acuña, *Occupied America: A History of Chicanos*, 2nd ed. (New York: Harper & Row, 1981); Mario Barrera, Alberto Camarillo, and Francisco Hernandez, eds., *Work, Family, Sex Roles, Language: The National Association for Chicano Studies, Selected Papers, 1979* (Berkeley: Tonatiuh-Quinto Sol, 1980); Mario T. García, "The Chicana in American History: The Mexican Women of El Paso, 1880–1920: A Case Study," *Pacific Historical Review* 49 (May 1980): 315–338; Juan Gonzales, *Harvest of Empire: A History of Latinos in America* (New York: Viking, 2000); Manuel G. Gonzales, *Mexicanos: A History of Mexicans in the United States* (Bloomington: Indiana University Press, 1999); Manuel G. Gonzales and Cynthia M. Gonzales, eds., *En Aquel Entonces: Readings in Mexican-American History* (Bloomington: Indiana University Press, 2000); Leo Grebler, et al., *The Mexican-American People: The Nation's Second Largest Minority* (New York: Free Press, 1970); Richard Griswold del Castillo and Arnoldo de León, *North to Aztlán: A History of Mexican Americans in the United States* (New York: Twayne, 1996); David G. Gutiérrez, *Walls and Mirrors: Mexican Americans, Mexican Immigrants, and the Politics of Ethnicity* (Berkeley: University of California Press, 1995); Alejandro Portes and Robert L. Bach, *Latin Journey: Cuban and Mexican Immigrants in the United States* (Berkeley: University of California Press, 1985); and George J. Sánchez, *Becoming Mexican American: Ethnicity, Culture, and Identity in Chicano Los Angeles, 1900–1945* (New York: Oxford University Press, 1993).

On Middle Eastern immigrants, see Eric J. Hooglund, ed., *Crossing the Waters: Arabic-Speaking Immigrants to the United States Before 1940* (Washington, D.C.: Smithsonian Institution Press, 1987); Gregory Orfalea, *Before the Flames: A Quest for the History of Arab Americans* (Austin: University of Texas Press, 1988); and Adele Younis, *The Coming of Arabic-Speaking People to the United States*, ed. Philip M. Kayal (New York: Center for Migration Studies, 1995).

On Scandinavian immigrants, see Adolph B. Beson and Naborth Hedin, eds., *Swedes in America, 1638–1938* (New Haven: Yale University Press, 1938); María Bjerg, "A Tale of Two Settlements: Danish Immigrants on the American Prairie and the Argentine Pampa, 1860–1930," *Annals of Iowa* 59 (Winter 200): 1–34; Sten Carlsson, *Swedes in North America: Technical, Cultural, and Political Achievements* (Stockholm: Streiffert, 1988); Odd S. Lovell, *The Promise of America: A History of the Norwegian-American People*, rev. ed. (Minneapolis: University of Minnesota Press, 1999); and Marion John Nelson, ed., *Material Culture and People's Art Among the Norwegians in America* (Northfield, Minn.: Norwegian-American Historical Association, 1994).

On southern and eastern European immigrants, see Karel D. Bicha, "Hunkies: Stereotyping the Slavic Immigrants, 1890–1920," *Journal of American Ethnic History* 2 (Fall 1982): 16–38; Waclaw Kruszka, *A History of the Poles in America to 1908*, ed. James S. Pula, trans. Krystyna Jankowski (Washington, D.C.: Catholic University of America Press, 1993); Myron B. Kuropas, *The Ukrainian Americans: Roots and Aspirations, 1884–1954* (Toronto: University of Toronto Press, 1991); Charles C. Moskos, *Greek Americans: Struggle and Success* (Englewood Cliffs, N.J.: Prentice-Hall, 1980); Richard Sallet, *Russian-German Settlements in the United States*, trans. Lauren J. Rippley and Armand Bauer (Fargo, N.D.: North Dakota Institute for Regional Studies, 1974); Theodore Saloutos, *The Greeks in the United States* (Cambridge: Harvard University Press, 1984); Orest Subtelny, *Ukrainians in North America: An Illustrated History* (Toronto: University of Toronto Press, 1991); and Helen Stankiewicz Zand, "Polish American Childways," *Polish American Studies* 16 (1959): 74–79.

Index

Japan, xi, 20, 167, 178
Japanese Americans, 170–171; internment
  policies against, 167
Japanese Association of America, 97
Japanese Humane Society of Los Angeles:
  Shonien, founding of, 50
Japanese immigrants, 40; and childbirth,
  27; discrimination against, 23, 24; and
  hara obi, 27; and Issei poems, 90; and
  Nisei, 98; and *samba*, 27
Japanese immigration, 10, 12; and Nisei, 50
Japanese language schools, 98, 99
Japanese Teachers Association of America,
  97
Jeong, Bessie, 123
Jewish Daily Forward, 73
Jewish education: and *cheder*, 96; and
  Jewish language schools, 97; and
  Talmud Torah schools, 96
Jewish immigration, 10
Jewish Messenger, 78
Jewish Training School, 108–109
Jews: Americanization, encouraging of, 74;
  and childbirth, 26; community
  institutions, Americanization in, 78; and
  education, 73; in garment industry, 11;
  and Holocaust, 167; mortality rate of,
  40
Johnson, Albert, 166
Johnson, Grove, 81
Judaism, 97
Juvenile courts, 7, 143

Kansparek, Joe and John, 144
Kaplan, Saul, 116
Kaster, Minnie, 158
Kawachi, Yoshito, 82
Keating-Owen Act, 115
Kekonnen, Peter, 155
Kindergarten movement, 21, 50, 52; and
  Americanization, 51, 53
Korean language schools, 97
Ku Klux Klan, 165

Language schools, 92; and
  Americanization, 101, 129;

Americanization, as detrimental to,
  189n60; categories of, 93; and Christian
  missionaries, 99; enrollment, drop in,
  169; and heritage schools, 93, 97; and
  nationalist schools, 93, 96; and parochial
  schools, 93, 94; and public
  schoolchildren, 101
Lasker, Bruno, 83
Lawrence (Mass.): textile workers' strike in,
  66
League of Nations: Declaration of the
  Rights of the Child, adoption of, 8
Leung, Lillie, 148, 156
L'Italia (newspaper), 74, 158
Little Italy, 11
Long, Tony, 86
Los Angeles (Calif.), 76, 84, 101, 116, 167
Lowe, Pardee, 30, 37, 70, 77, 98, 106;
  discrimination against, 148
Lowe, Thomas Riley Marshall, 30
Lowe, Woodrow Wilson, 30
Lowell (Mass.), 38, 114
Lukin, Samuel, 158
Lum, Martha, 82
Lum v. Rice, 82
Lutheran churches: and vacation schools,
  95

Madich, Steve, 115
Maine, 35
Mangione, Jerre, 86
Massachusetts Immigration Commission,
  95
Massachusetts Society for Prevention of
  Cruelty to Children, 144
Mass immigration, 177; economic
  opportunity, as crucial, 178. *See also*
  Immigration.
McCormick, Cyrus, 3, 4
Mendoza, Isabella, 155
Mexican Americans: ethnic identity of, 170
Mexican immigration, 9, 10, 12
Mexican Revolution, 9, 166
Mexicans, 11; discrimination toward, 170;
  hostility toward, 82; and repatriation
  policy, 170; in United States, 167, 170

A NOTE ON THE AUTHOR

Melissa R. Klapper was born in Miami, Florida, and studied American history at Goucher College and Rutgers University, where she received a Ph.D. She has written widely on matters of immigration and ethnicity in American life, including *Jewish Girls Coming of Age in America, 1860–1920*. She is now associate professor of history at Rowan University in Glassboro, New Jersey.